Fortress   Architecture and Military History in Malta

FORTRESS

Architecture and Military History in Malta

Quentin Hughes
Professor of Architecture in the Royal University of Malta

With photographs by David Wrightson

Lund Humphries · London

Copyright © 1969 Lund Humphries
First edition 1969
Published by Lund Humphries, 12 Bedford Square London WC1

Designed by Herbert Spencer and Hansje Oorthuys

Made and printed in Great Britain by
Lund Humphries, Bradford & London

To Margaret

Acknowledgements

Most of the illustrations in this book are reproduced from photographs by David Wrightson and the author which were taken during a visit to the island made possible by the generous assistance of the Malta Government Tourist Board to whom the publishers wish to express their gratitude.

Photographs by David Wrightson: pages 11, 12, 18, 19, 21, 22 (top), 29, 33–38, 43, 59, 60, 63, 72, 76, 80, 82–85, 87–90, 93–98, 100–103, 105, 107, 112, 119, 124, 125, 127–129, 131, 135, 138, 139, 141–145, 147, 153, 155–157, 159–163, 165, 172–185, 187–190, 192, 193, 197–199, 201–203, 205, 209, 210, 213–216, 218–224, 245, 246, 250, 252, 253, 256, 257, 269

Photographs by the author: pages 13, 20, 22 (bottom), 110, 133, 137, 150, 152, 158, 168–171, 195, 196, 200, 212, 225, 228, 240, 241, 243, 244, 249, 258

The publishers express their thanks to the following for permission to reproduce other subjects: Alec Tiranti Ltd, London (Quentin Hughes, *Building of Malta*, 1956): pages 86, 89, 104; Bethell, John, St. Albans: pages 272, 273, 275; British Museum, London: pages 46, 65; Ellis, R., Malta: pages 242, 255; Encyclopaedia Britannica: page 237; Imperial War Museum, London: pages 260, 267; Landstrom, Bjorn, Bokforlaget Forum, Stockholm: pages 27, 231; Royal Malta Library: pages 115, 116, 121

Signora Costanza Laparelli-Pitti kindly lent a copy of the Codex Laparelli which Sig. Nino Pranzo-Zaccaria of Milan helped to translate.

Contents

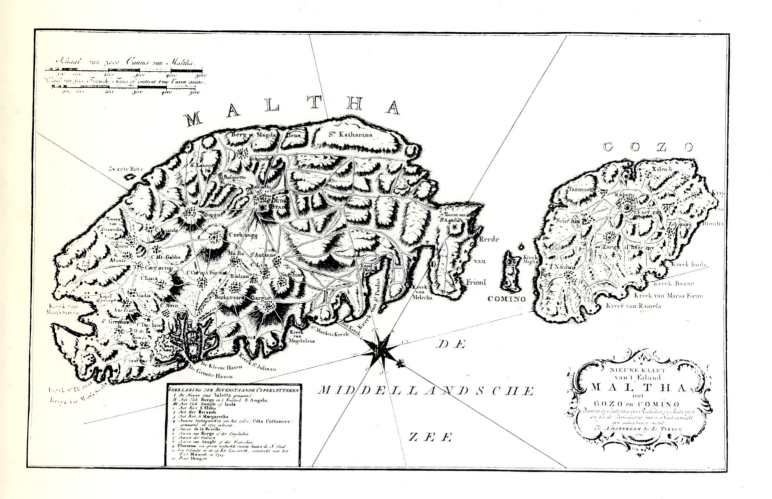

Introduction

Map of Malta and Gozo printed in Amsterdam by Is Tirion in 1761.

This is a different place. The first impact on the visitor is one of surprise, for this is not like the Mediterranean coast, nor is it just a group of rocky islands. Generations of Maltese have cut, scooped out, and piled great masses of stone so that the place seems a conglomeration of cubic shapes. Form is paramount. The ingredient is a soft limestone which can be easily hewn and planed into rectangular shapes. Stone on stone rise from the rock, the man-made edifices scarcely distinguishable from the virgin ground. All the houses are flat-roofed and cubic and seem like an extension of the cliff strata. Mile upon mile of fortified curtain and bastion rise inevitably from the solid ground and seem an integral aspect of the scene.

The archipelago is small. Malta, a bare seventeen miles long and nine miles broad is shaped like a lozenge, with Gozo, about half the size, lying to the north-west. There are two islands in the channel between Malta and Gozo, and another, Filfla, is sufficiently distant from the south-west coast-line to offer a useful artillery and bombing target. The group of islands lies at the crossroads of the Mediterranean, halfway between Gibraltar and Suez. The routes have been traversed from earliest times by a continuous traffic of traders and conquerors, with the result that Malta and her smaller sisters have been in the path of many races and have, throughout history, inevitably become the pawn of their power games. For the Maltese self-preservation has always been the first requisite, and the need to bolt and hide in caves or holes scooped out from the soft stone ground became almost a reflex action. A more powerful occupying power or conqueror could bring some measure of security and peace, but the best protection was afforded by the build-up of long lines of defence and an intricate system of fortification. Look-out towers gave warning, forts guarded the bays and creeks, castles gave some measure of protection to the wealthy who dwelt in the countryside, and miles of outworks, bastions, cavaliers, and curtain walls were spun around the main centres of population. This has resulted in one of the most complex *enceintes* in the history of military architecture.

The fortifications are functional. They arose out of an urgent need for protection and consequently they display a sense of integration with the landscape which characterizes the best products of Man. The Maltese fortifications illustrate a part of the story of the great struggle between the Islamic and Christian worlds when a clash of ideologies threw up a barrier

A Maltese fishing Luzzu in the harbour at Mgarr.

more impenetrable than any modern 'iron curtain'. Life within the defensive ring became comparatively safe. The native population grew and prospered and visitors came from most of the Western countries, bringing with them their ideas, tastes, and languages. The result is an extraordinary amalgam of national characteristics within a very small area of land. The architecture of Malta, its churches, palaces, villas, houses, and fortifications, provides a visual illustration of these characteristics.

However, although enriched by European culture, the general appearance of the island, which is imparted by the closely huddled houses of the villages and the scattered farmhouses in the countryside, is peculiarly Maltese and has an indigenous quality which is striking when one considers the small

Maltese fishing boats at Marsaxlokk.

land area of Malta and Gozo. If the form of things is paramount in Malta it is because at first this is the only quality which is distinguishable. A brilliant sun strikes off the bleached stone throwing its edges and corners into dark shade. Everywhere there is a contrast of light and shade. Blinding terraces of wall stretch endlessly across the countryside. Villages rise like piled-up lumps of yellow sugar, sharp-edged, flat-roofed, and cubic.

At first it would seem that the Maltese love of colour has been inhibited by the brilliance of the sunlight. But this is not so. It has been channelled into carefully selected areas and on to objects where maximum impact can be obtained. Dghajsas and Luzzus, those graceful Maltese fishing boats, have for generations been painted in rich contrasting shades of red, blue, and yellow. The result is a folk art practised with considerable confidence and verve. The rich contrasts of colour can also be seen on buses and lorries delicately ornamented with lineal patterns in gold and silver. Until the recent and disastrous introduction of colour on the façades of buildings, Maltese houses have traditionally been content to display natural stone or cream colour wash. Colour had been relegated to the interiors, where the full impact could be felt. The insides of cathedrals, churches, palaces, and villas provided scenes of riotous colour embossed with gold – a richness and splendour of expression rarely matched elsewhere. It is as though the people were starved of external colour where the sun beats mercilessly on the stone-work reducing walls to a blinding whiteness, and sought compensation in the cool shade of the interiors. Consequently, much of the richness of the Maltese scene is not revealed to the casual eye, and it takes time and patience to penetrate to the greenery of courtyard and walled garden and the intricate colour of church and house which lie behind the plain stone walls of the street façades. A variety of plants grow in profusion hidden from the passer-by yet providing the owner with a luxurious retreat from the heat of the summer sun.

Malta is still a place of controlled contrasts. Where, through the exuberant expression of individualism and the unbridled use of advertisement, the Western World has over-indulged itself, thereby destroying the impact of contrast, the Maltese have, until recently, maintained this delicate balance. The impact of a Maltese Baroque church is heightened by its setting among a cluster of small, plain, tight-packed houses. The graceful modelled domes and towers of the parish churches stand out above the lower groups of flat-roofed buildings. The powerful shapes of the massive coastal forts dominate the craggy outline of the coast. The high plain surfaces of the Valletta fortifications seem to form a plinth for the lace-like intricacies of her baroque palaces and churches. The still waters of the creeks and harbours are a table upon which stand the involved architectural masses of Malta's coastal towns. Throughout history, Malta has manifested a strong preoccupation with the use of contrast. After the sullen days of waiting, the sudden flash of arms. From the uneasy peace, a brilliant barrage of tracer shells bursting over the Grand Harbour. In the silence of the hot summer nights the black sky exploding into a brilliance of colour from the fireworks of the festas.

This is indeed a different place – a place which must be known to be understood and understood to be enjoyed.

Chapter 1: The Island of Antiquity

From time immemorial, the Maltese islands have been the scene of monumental building. Far back in the darkness beyond history, men built, scooped out of the ground, or piled up large masses of carved stones, these so effectively arranged that they still strike us today as impressive. On Malta and Gozo there are the remains of a group of Megalithic temples of great importance, Ħaġar Qim, Mnajdra, Hal Saflieni and Ggantija. We do not know where the race that built them came from, where it went, and why it disappeared so suddenly leaving its temples as evidence of its existence. Strange cart tracks also remain, running for distances on the hard rock ledges of the highlands, sometimes dropping sheer into the sea. Undoubtedly these are the remnants of some system of communications; the deep ruts were perhaps worn in the stone by sledge-like carts. One can imagine shafts attached to horses or oxen and laden with heavy stones, the shaft ends resting on the ground and being dragged along, thus gradually eroding the surface of the stone. The tracks provide graphic evidence of the theory that Malta was once attached to the mainland of Europe. It seems likely that at one time a great earthquake ravaged the central Mediterranean, splitting the rock so that the sea gushed between Sicily and Malta separating the two lands for ever, and perhaps also breaking a land link with the North African coast.

These early buildings took advantage of the quality of the Maltese stone, a limestone easily cut and fashioned, and ideal for building purposes. The rooms of the temples were scooped out or built up in concentric circles – their ceilings roofed with corbelled stones like the beehive Treasury of Atrius at Mycenae on the southern coast of Greece. It should be remembered that the spaces in the temples were meant to be appreciated as an interior progression and not seen exposed from above: all the rooms were either below the natural surface of the rock, or were covered over with stones and soil. This was an architecture of space, foreshadowing the Roman achievement of the baths and the basilicas, certainly in intention if not in scale. The occupants, probably priests, passed in procession from room to room. These rooms, whose sites were matched with balancing apses, were symmetrical, and carefully proportioned. Each major room was linked to its successor by a bridge-passage, and the whole scheme of the design involved a mystical harmony.

Model of Tarxien temple in the Valletta Museum.

The temples vary in size and complexity. Tarxien occupies an area of about 6500 square yards. Ħaġar Qim has stones twenty-two feet long and weighing many tons. At Ggantija in Gozo there stands the most impressive of the surviving monuments with its largest chamber, once richly painted in bright red, measuring thirty-five feet in length by thirty feet across.

The insistence upon the use of curved shapes is the most remarkable feature of these early Maltese builders. Straight lines and sharp angles are rare, and everywhere are to be found soft sweeping curves: in the overall disposition of the room shapes, in the walls and roofs themselves, and in the spiral patterns which, with great delicacy, decorate many of these walls. Long, curving, interwoven shapes are articulated with round chisel holes,

Model of the Ggantija temples at Gozo, in the Valletta Museum.

the masons inspired, like the artists of the Japanese prints, by crests of the wave and sea-blown surf. There is, too, a remarkable unity in the work of these men; the stone-cutters of buildings and sculpture share the same aesthetic – the fat female figures, personifying fertility, are cut from rock or modelled in clay. Large bulging slabs of flesh, soft rolling curves, grotesque yet strangely fascinating, are products of the mind that fashioned the entrance to Haġar Qim. The affinity can quickly be perceived. Each stone is carefully selected and carefully cut; the corners are rounded and the edges curved back. The verticals are not quite vertical but pitched slightly in, revealing that extraordinary quality of monumentality which is so evident in the sculptured figures of this period.[1]

There is no reason to connect these primitive people with the modern Maltese. Their remarkable civilization was wiped out, but whether by plague or by attack from a more powerful enemy we do not know. Certainly there is no evidence of defence, no fort or castle, to suggest that these were a warlike people. The evidence is to the contrary, although it would be going too far on existing evidence to suggest that this was a lotus-eating community. But its architecture ceased suddenly because it had no seed, or so it appeared, for it was replaced by a harsher, cruder zigzag pattern of sculpture and architecture, probably the product of a more war-like race. Yet

when one looks at the rich products of Maltese Baroque, the exquisite curvature of the carved stone and the internal modelling of space which flowered in the hands of sixteenth-century Maltese craftsmen, one can be forgiven for wondering if the experience was drawn from an ancient, long-forgotten heritage.

Was there any direct link? Not at first sight, though some of the Megalithic temples were known and mentioned by writers from the mid-seventeenth century onwards. Serious archaeological excavation did not begin until the nineteenth century, and there is still much to unearth. In a glass case in the Valletta Museum, there is a very small stone model of a Megalithic building said to date from the Mġair phase, about 2800 B.C. The model portrays a single-cell stone building constructed of carefully shaped rectangular stones with rounded edges. The building is approximately circular, and the walls slope in slightly so that they can be spanned by long, single slabs of sandstone. As these roof slabs span right across the chamber, it is evident that the model depicts a building of modest dimensions, probably no more than about ten feet from wall to wall. Is it not possible that this is a model of a contemporary house? The belief that a house is a little temple, or a temple a great house, runs right back in history to the origins of architecture. If this is a house, then it is conceivable that the evidence of actual examples has disappeared. Small structures like this standing above the level of the ground would have been cleared to make space for new buildings and their stones used for fresh constructions. It would have been remarkable if any such houses had survived. In Malta, however, a building type has persisted which shows remarkable similarity to the Megalithic single-cell building and which continued to be built until quite recently. The little beehive shelters sometimes found in the fields of central and northern Malta are used by farmers for sheltering sheep and goats, small conical structures not built of dressed limestone but constructed for convenience from the irregular shaped stones found in the fields. The huts are usually about five feet in diameter and their walls curve so that the domical roof can be constructed of overlapping stones. Would it be presumptive to suggest that these are the descendants of the Maltese Megalithic houses? In south-east Italy, conical houses still abound. In the town of Alberobello, and in the country around Noci and Putignano, clusters of these buildings are still in use.

The fat ladies of Malta. A prehistoric statue from Ħaġar Qim now preserved in the Valletta Museum.

Model of a small Megalithic building dating from about 2800 B.C., now in the Valletta Museum.

From classical times other civilizations have left their imprint on Malta. The Greeks, who called the place Melita – the 'honeyed one' – came, may even have colonized and then departed with some rapidity, driven out by the trading Carthaginians. Romans started visiting the island from about 480 B.C. and were in full occupation from 216 B.C. They have left their stamp – order, organization, system – features evident in the remains of their architecture on Malta, remains which are found in the villas at Rabat and Ghajn Tuffieha. The residue of Roman art shows high sophistication, in particular in the optical disturbances their artists created in the still well-preserved floors of the villas. There is an extraordinary illusionistic effect of alternating progression and recession, creating an ambiguity of the third dimension. As Gombrich has written, describing a similar mosaic at Roman Antioch, 'We can read each of the units as a solid cube lighted from above, or as a hollow cube lighted from below'.[2] This is the sort of illusionistic trick which is carried to extremes in the Fraser spiral where complete circular rings appear to spiral towards a vortex – the basis of Op Art demonstrated some 2000 years ago.

In A.D.395 Malta passed under the jurisdiction of the Eastern Empire at Constantinople, until it was captured in 807 by the Arabs. Little building evidence remains to recall their stay. The departure of the Arabs was precipitated by the arrival of a striking force from Sicily led by Count Roger the Norman who occupied the islands in 1090. From then on, Malta and Gozo have remained a Christian stronghold, often menaced by Islamic invasion but never completely conquered. It is worth noting that about this time, merchants from Amalfi set up a hospital in Jerusalem to succour pilgrims on their way to the Holy City. Gerard, first rector of the hospital, formed a religious body bound by vows of poverty, chastity, and obedience and subject to the jurisdiction of the Patriarch of Jerusalem. It was later, in 1113, that Pascal II sanctioned its establishment as a religious order and Raymond Du Puy, Gerard's successor at the hospital, extended the activity of the Order to cover the protection of pilgrims journeying from the sea to Jerusalem. This was the beginning of the military Brotherhood of the Hospitallers, The Order of St John of Jerusalem, which was later to play such a part in forging the destiny of Malta.

Norman, Saubian, Angevin, and Aragonese all occupied the island in turn, leaving their palaces to stand in the old city called Mdina perched on the high ground in the centre of the island. Meanwhile, scooped out of the solid rock, troglodyte churches, their origin obscured in antiquity, continued to be built. Underground churches and catacombs abound, and many lie buried beneath later buildings. Some, isolated, remote and superseded by later churches which replaced them, still contain traces of fresco. Others, where particular veneration was attached to them, were incorporated beneath new churches like St Paul's at Rabat.[3]

Maltese limestone yields easily to the axe, saw, and chisel, and has at all times been the basic material for the construction of buildings. The upper layer, termed globigerina, is an ideal material for rich carving. It indurates on exposure, forming a hard-wearing surface, but it is susceptible to salt winds and spray so that in an exposed position the deeper stratum of coralline stone has to be used. Alternatively, the lower stories of buildings are often colour-washed to prevent erosion. The stone cuts easily into cubes and can be seen stacked in the fields ready for use. As a result, the indigenous architecture which emerges is cubic. Flat-roofed, rectangular constructions, clustered and piled together, give an extraordinary homogeneous character to the islands, a fitting field for sculpture and a suitable background for the elaborate development of the flowing form of the Baroque church.[4]

[1] Evans (J. D.) *Malta* (London 1959) gives a valuable assessment of the archaeology of the islands.
[2] Gombrich (E. H.) *Art and Illusion* (London and New York 1960), page 266. For Roman examples in Malta see 'Roman villa and thermae at Ghajn Tuffieha – Malta' in *Bulletin of the Museum* (Valletta February 1931), pages 56–64.
[3] Leopardi (E. R.) 'Troglodyte Churches', in *Sunday Times of Malta* (14 August 1965), lists many of them.
   Golcher (O. F.) 'Mdina – the ancient capital – From Troglodytes to the Knights' in *Sunday Times of Malta* (19 October 1958).
[4] Jones (Harry D.) 'Memoranda and Details of the Mode of Building Houses, etc. in the island of Malta' in *Papers on Subjects connected with the duties of the Corps of Royal Engineers*, Volume 5 (London 1842). A complete study of Maltese materials and traditional methods of construction. See also Harrison (Austin St B.) and Hubbard (R. Pearse S.) 'Maltese Vernacular' in *Architectural Review*, Volume 105, No.626 (February 1949), pages 77–80.

Chapter 2: The Great Siege

The Knights of St John of Jerusalem, sometimes known as the Hospitallers, were founded as a religious brotherhood during the first Crusade. In Jerusalem they had built a hospital where they cared for sick pilgrims visiting the holy places. From a comparatively early period they acted as armed contingents to defend the pilgrims on the routes to these cities, but it was not until the early thirteenth century that the Brotherhood became a para-military organization dedicated to the task of defending the Holy Land against Muslim invaders. Because of the scarcity of Christian troops, more and more reliance had to be placed upon effective defensive positions and gradually the Knights acquired fortresses from private landlords and developed them into the great concentric citadels of the Holy Land. Beit Jibrin was taken over in 1137, Krak des Cavaliers in 1142 (held until 1271), and Margrat was occupied and extended in 1186 to become the headquarters of the Order until it, too, was lost in 1285. Because of the shortage of manpower, impregnable sites had to be chosen and exploited. Strong keeps built after the manner of the French castles became a feature of these fortresses, and concentric rings of defences, built one inside the other and rising higher and higher, were constructed, so that those defending the outer walls were covered by fire from positions behind and above them. The danger of this sort of military thinking was that it created a reliance upon passive defence. There was usually only one small entrance to the castle and this made it very difficult for the defending forces to carry out a sortie as an effective counter-attack. If the entrance could be defended by one man, T. E. Lawrence shrewdly pointed out that 'it could certainly be besieged by two standing on each side of the doorway to prevent egress'.[1] The Christian defence of the Holy Land gradually collapsed and, with the fall of Acre, the last stronghold, in 1291, the Knights withdrew, first to Cyprus and then to the island of Rhodes. Rhodes, that pleasant green land in the Aegean, lay under the nose of the Turkish power and on the trade route between Constantinople, last stronghold of the Roman empire in the east, and the states of western Christendom, a trade route that had flourished for over two centuries. The Hospitallers' security was often threatened and when Constantinople fell in 1453 their position as a forward post gradually became untenable. In 1523 the Turks mounted a major assault on the island and, after a prolonged siege, the Knights were forced to come to honourable terms and were permitted to evacuate the island, embark on their ships, and take with them their belongings and many of the Greek inhabitants. After years of tiresome negotiation the Grand Master of the Order, Philippe Villiers de l'Isle Adam, persuaded Charles V, King of Spain, to grant to the Knights the islands of Malta and Gozo, which were to become their head-quarters until attacked by Napoleon Bonaparte in 1798. The gift was not without its strings. Charles also required the Knights to take over the fort-ress of Tripoli, built insecurely on shifting sand, a desert outpost defending his north African possessions. With some misgivings the Knights accepted the gift of Malta. The island was barren and seemed inhospitable after the lush vegetation of Rhodes. However, their acceptance of the offer and their occupation of Malta and Gozo were to have the most profound effect upon the growth and visual development of these islands. No other circumstance in the long history of Maltese growth has been so significant and so far reaching.

When the Knights arrived in Malta on 26 October 1530, they were, in addition to being consummate fortress builders, the possessors of one of the most aggressive fleets in the eastern Mediterranean. Their naval striking power depended upon their possession and development of a number of fast galleys, the sixteenth-century equivalent of the modern destroyer. Galleys were oar-propelled, moved by the sweating, manacled ranks of hard-driven slaves lashed to a pitch of frenzy when the last ounce of speed was required from these fast vessels. Their hulls were long and low, their decks easily swamped in choppy weather so that they were really summer-weather boats, not venturing into the Mediterranean during the winter months. In design,

they were the end of a long line of development from Greek and Roman days, development which had brought refinements in the same manner as the breeding of greyhounds. These galleys were very fast for short spurts and once they came within striking range of heavy cargo vessels they made them an easy prey. For cruising they used a large lateen sail amidships, similar to those still used on the modern Gozo boats. Galleys were used by both sides and the galleys of the Order were pennanted and richly decorated, probably the sleekest boats ever designed. They were long and lean, often reaching to nearly 100 feet. On their bows they had a powerful ramming device which could cut clean through another vessel, and above the ram was mounted a heavy cannon or coursier to blast a passage forward.[2] These vessels were the cavalry of the seas and the Knights' naval strike force. They ranged far out into the Mediterranean looting the Turkish-held islands which became a happy hunting ground for rich booty. These expeditions were pleasantly called caravans. To the galley captain fell the lot of equipping the ship, funds for which had often to be recouped from proceeds made in the capture of Turkish boats. Conditions on board were cramped, smelly, and often uncomfortable, so that it is little wonder that the Knights grew in time to display a swashbuckling attitude when on land and sought recompense for their naval existence in stylish and comfortable living at home.

If the Knights' striking power lay in the use and development of fast galleys, their defensive strategy was based on the maintenance of permanent lines of defence designed to be held by a comparatively small army. Their engineers were continuously experimenting with ways to improve defences and already in the fifteenth century the Superintendent of Fortifications, Pierre d'Aubusson of Auvergne, had conceived the idea of building a simple bastion, forerunner of the projecting bulwark system which was to become such a characteristic of the defences of Valletta and the Three Cities.[3] In Rhodes an elementary bastion had been introduced to replace the earlier system of circular towers placed at intervals along a line of curtain walling and the Italian engineers of the late fifteenth century, men like Francesco di Giorgio Martini, were forced to refine this invention after the catastrophic defeat of the Italian forces by the invading army of Charles VIII. In 1494 Charles's army marched the length of the Italian peninsula cracking open antiquated fortresses like so many ripe nuts. A bastion consists of a triangular projection pushed out from the main curtain wall of the fortification to which it is joined by two nibs. In these nibs, called flanks, guns are placed so that they can pour enfilade or raking fire along each face of the bastion, that is, two sides of the triangle. Any attacking troops were then forced to pass through this field of fire before reaching the face of the bastion, which in turn had to be captured before the curtain wall could be attacked. The angles of the triangle were worked out so that every inch of the bastion was under direct observation from the gunners and could be covered by their fire. This idea of pushing forward a portion of the fortified wall in the form of a bastion was the beginning of the defence in depth which became the main contribution of baroque fortification.

When the Knights arrived in Malta many were depressed by the prospect of life there, where the sun bounced off the yellow limestone and conditions in the summer months seemed almost unbearable. Their Commissioners had warned them of the prospects when they visited the Islands in 1524. 'Malta', they said, 'has a population of about 12,000 inhabitants, the greatest part of whom are poor and miserable owing to the barrenness of the soil and the frequent descents of the corsairs who, without the smallest sentiment or compassion, carry off all the unfortunate Maltese who happen to fall into their hands. In a word, a residence in Malta appears extremely disagreeable, indeed, almost insupportable, particularly in the summer.' Gozo, with about

An early map of Malta, showing Mdina, the old capital, as a walled town, a fort on the peninsula at St Angelo, and numerous villages scattered about the island.

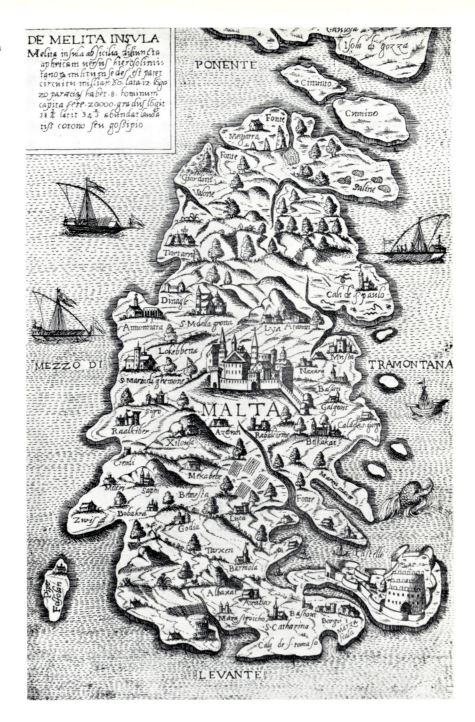

5000 inhabitants, appeared more fertile, but had no suitable harbours so it could hardly be used as a main base for the Knights. However, it was considered advisable to occupy this northern island in case the Turks should land there and use it as a springboard for an attack on Malta. The great merits of Malta lay in its strategic position commanding the main channel through which all shipping between the eastern and western Mediterranean must pass, and its fine harbours. In addition to having a number of spacious bays, there were deep landlocked harbours, protected from the fierce, sudden Mediterranean gales, grouped in a cluster around the little port of Il Borgo. The old capital, then called Città Notabile and now known as Mdina, lay in the centre of the island on high ground. There lived the Maltese nobility, who resented the arrival of the Knights, for not only did this place them in a position of inferiority, but it also ran counter to the agreement made with the Spanish Emperor in 1428 which guaranteed them the freedom of the island. They withdrew to their palaces in the old city and lived in piqued isolation.

But Città Notabile was unsuitable as a headquarters for the seafaring Knights of St John. Instead they chose the small hamlet of Il Borgo which lay on the central promontory which runs out into the Grand Harbour from the eastern mainland. Undoubtedly this base was chosen because already there was a small fort on the top of the peninsula and sufficient buildings to provide at least a temporary shelter until new ones could be built. The deep inlets now called Kalkara and Dockyard creeks provided protected shelter and safe anchorage for the galleys. The two promontories, upon which are now built Vittoriosa and Senglea, had comparatively short land fronts and therefore did not require elaborate and expensive defence works. There were, however, grave disadvantages in this choice of site which were to imperil the safety of the defenders in the great siege that followed. Both promontories were overlooked by higher ground: from the south-west by the Corradino heights and from the north-west by the long spit of land called Mount Sceberras, upon which the city of Valletta was later built. Beyond this land lay a further haven called Marsamxett which, if Mount Sceberras were captured by an attacking force, could be used for a safe and convenient harbour by the Turkish armada. A small fort, St Elmo, placed on the very tip of the Sceberras peninsula was all that barred entry to Marsamxett harbour. The name St Elmo had at some time been bastardized from St Ermo, patron saint of sailors, to whom the little chapel on the point had been dedicated. The remains of the chapel were incorporated into the fabric of the star-shaped fort which was later built there by the Knights, and the remains are still visible.

The existing fortifications were rudimentary – when the Knights arrived a small fort called St Angelo mounted two guns on the tip of the Borgo peninsula covering the waters of the Grand Harbour, and there was a watch tower on the coast of the Sceberras peninsula.

In 1530 Il Borgo was no more than a hamlet of close-packed, single or two-storied houses clustered along the water's edge and beneath the walls of the small fortress. All the houses had flat roofs, a feature which must have struck new recruits as odd and uncivilized, for flat-roof construction is comparatively rare in Europe. The flat roof was, and remains to this day, almost ubiquitous on the island of Malta, with the use of the slightly pitched roof being confined to some churches and civic buildings. In spite of the fact that this flat-roof form of construction was labelled primitive by most contemporary writers, it was the only feasible solution to the problem in Malta where timber has always been expensive because it had to be imported from the mainland of Europe. To overcome this shortage of timber Maltese builders used slabs of stone which were laid on to internal arches. The arches had to be placed about four feet apart as the stone slabs were capable of spanning only that distance. The edges of the stone slabs were bevelled and the triangular-shaped groove which was left between the edges was filled with small pebbles soaked in water. Three or four inches of dry chippings were laid on top and these were covered with another layer mixed with lime mortar. When the surface had been well rammed down a mixture of diffone, which consists of small pieces of broken earthenware pots mixed with lime and water, was beaten into a paste and laid uniformly over the whole surface of the roof. The process of beating and ramming went on until all the excess water was squeezed out, then finally the surface of the roof was divided into strips, each about two and a half feet wide, and a woman, seated on a small stool and barefoot, took each strip. Working with her partners, she swept the surface of the roof with towels, smoothing and glazing it, so that eventually a perfectly impervious and waterproof surface was obtained. This is a very remarkable form of construction as it is able to withstand the torrential rain and wind of winter and the blistering sun of the long dry summers.

It is so successful that even today it is still used in exactly the same way. Far from being a primitive form of construction it is a most highly sophisticated method of finishing and waterproofing a building and Francesco Laparelli, the Italian engineer who designed Valletta, was one of the first to realize its significance when he wrote a short treatise on the development of the art of building.[4]

'Other writers have shown', he said, 'as examples of primitive cities those with buildings roofed in mud and have said that the inhabitants were of a lower intelligence and were ignorant of what others had done. What would these ancient and modern writers say about Malta, where people come with many languages bringing with them a knowledge of what is done elsewhere? In this island they use compressed earth and mud to cover the roofs of their houses. This is very good. Everywhere people use what nature gives them and here nature has offered a strong white earth which can be used to cover the houses.'

The Knights took over many of the existing buildings and improved them by adding embellishments to the façades and refurbishing the interiors. The demand for property far exceeded the supply, and a tribunal called the Officio delle Case was set up whose main purpose was to fix a fair rent for houses and shops. Workmen were brought over from Sicily to swell the ranks of the building trades, and speed the repair of old buildings and the building of new. It is perhaps strange that so little architectural influence from Sicily appears evident during these early years of the Knights' residence in Malta. However, it may be that, with the architectural control in the hands of immigrants from Rhodes, a conservative attitude to design prevailed. There is evidence to suggest that Nicolo de Flavari was the first architect of the Order in their residence on Malta. From a letter in the Archives of Malta it would seem that Flavari left his wife and children 'to the great dangers of the Infidel who held Rhodes',[5] so that he might serve the Knights in Malta. One would love to know the details of this event. Was it a sacrifice on his part or an escape from family responsibilities? The letter refers to his love of the Order and one wonders if this were not perhaps greater than his love for his family. At all events he served the Order faithfully for a score of years until in 1555 he was thrown over as being too old and outmoded in his ways in favour of Nicola Belavante. Belavante stayed the course for only two years and one senses the frustration of the Knights searching

The auberge or hostel of the Knights from Auvergne, France and Provence in Il Borgo.

desperately for a competent modern architect to direct the expansion of their town and the creation of their public buildings. Genga was a comparatively important Italian architect of sufficient merit to receive attention in the pages of Vasari's *Lives of the Painters, Sculptors and Architects*. His services were in considerable demand and, whilst working in Rome, his help was sought by the Genoese for some of their fortifications. When the Duke of Urbino was created Pope Julius IV he was visited by two Knights who pleaded with him for several months in an effort to obtain the services of Bartolomeo Genga in Malta. Vasari records that they wanted Genga to fortify the island against the Turks and 'make two cities by uniting several scattered villages'. This must refer to Il Borgo (now Vittoriosa) and Isola (now Senglea).

Eventually the mission was successful and Bartolomeo 'set out with the Knights on the 20th January, 1558, but being delayed in Sicily by the fortune of the sea they did not reach Malta before the 14th March, where the Grand Master received them gladly. When shown what to do, Bartolomeo made fortifications of the utmost excellence so that he seemed a new Archimedes to the Grand Master and the Knights, who made him rich presents and greatly esteemed him'.[6]

Vasari tells how Genga made a model of a city, some churches and a palace for the Grand Master in beautiful style, and in Malta he died in July 1559 at the age of 43.

The auberges and the various buildings of the Knights which date from the period of Flavari's office are decorated with strange bulbous rolling mouldings which are locally referred to as 'fat' mouldings. Their origin is obscure and there is certainly nothing like them in Italy. These bulbous 'fat' mouldings are used on the surrounds of windows and doors, under cornices and sills and they continued to be built until about 1620 both in some of the less avant garde buildings in the new city of Valletta and, as one might expect, in the scattered country villages. Their origin is obscure; there does not seem to be anything similar on Rhodes and one may assume that they caused some embarrassment to the more elegant members of the Order who had a smattering of European sensibility. In the work executed in the last few years before the Turkish assault, important buildings like the Magisterial palace and the little chapel of St Anne, they give way to a new decoration, still backward by Florentine and Roman taste, but unquestionably

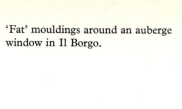
'Fat' mouldings around an auberge window in Il Borgo.

Italian in origin. This change is probably influenced by the advent of Bartolomeo Genga. In Rhodes the Knights' buildings had been segregated from other habitations, screened behind a high wall in an area reserved exclusively for them and termed a collachio. Because of the difficulty of pressing into use existing property, little of which was suitable for its task, the Knights were never able to regain this exclusiveness of residence. A collachio area was defined in Il Borgo, though it was not used exclusively by the Knights. It merely gave them the option to purchase or rent property from the Maltese. More will be said about the collachio system during the building of the new city of Valletta as it has considerable bearing on the design of that city. Il Borgo consisted of narrow, twisting streets, similar to Rhodes and many of the towns of the Greek islands, and was easy to defend by those who knew it well. It was a far cry from the town planning theory of the Italian Renaissance which favoured regularity, straight streets, and amply proportioned public squares. In addition to modernizing and building auberges, the Knights set about the task of construction of the Holy Infirmary in 1532 and the building was completed with extraordinary rapidity within one year. It was built to very high standards and proved a blessing during the great siege when, under impeccable hygienic conditions, many of the defenders were nursed back to health, whereas most of those similarly wounded in the Turkish camp succumbed to sickness. The Bishop built himself a palace in

Fort St Angelo across the waters of the Grand Harbour.

1542 and the Grand Master began the construction of the Magisterial palace on the heights of Fort St Angelo in 1555. The building was probably designed by Belavante and completed under the direction of Bartolomeo Genga.[7]

The main task of the Knights was to strengthen the defences of Malta and it was to this end that the best advice was sought. Four places needed to be reinforced: the fort of St Angelo which was the headquarters of the Order of St John; the tip of the Sceberras peninsula, which needed a new fortress; the southern land flank, which also required a strong fort; and a continuous line of fortifications to encircle the two towns of Il Borgo (Vittoriosa) and Isola (Senglea). St Angelo commanded the southern side of the

Grand Harbour and protected the two towns against attack from the sea. The fort needed rebuilding and enlarging and it is partly because of its situation on the spit of land and partly because it was the first fortification to be undertaken by the Knights in Malta that its design is more traditional than the other forts. It was encircled by a ring of high walls protected by towers and is in many ways similar to the Knights' Crusader castles and the citadel they raised at Rhodes. Even the idea of building the Grand Master's palace on the high point of the fort stems from the concept of designing a keep as the final point of defence.[8] On the landward side a cavalier, which is really a high-raised platform, dominated the houses in Il Borgo should they be captured. The great merit of the cavalier was that it was protected by a lower wall which projected in front of it, and should some of its walls crumble from enemy bombardment the masonry would not fall into the ditch and provide a bridge over which the enemy forces could attack. We are fortunate in possessing a series of engravings which faithfully reproduce the Maltese defences at the time of the Turkish attack of 1560. Eleven years after the siege was raised the Knights sent to Rome for an artist capable of depicting the great battle. Matteo Perez d'Aleccio, a Spanish painter, came to Malta in 1576 and painted the frescoes which adorn the Magisterial palace in Valletta. The scenes were subsequently engraved and published in Rome in 1582, with a later and better edition produced by Antonio Lucini of Florence in 1631.[9]

The tip of the Sceberras peninsula afforded a considerable problem. Any fort there would have to stand on its own for as long as possible in order to prevent the Turks entering the harbour of Marsamxett, or making a frontal attack on the Grand Harbour. For this reason it had to be on the tip of the peninsula, but it suffered from the disadvantage that it was overlooked by higher ground on Mount Sceberras. The term 'mount' is perhaps an exaggeration. The ground of the ridge rises in no place higher than 180 feet (at the Castille heights) and the main plateau, upon which St John's co-cathedral was later built and where the main Turkish batteries were entrenched, is only about 145 feet above the waters of the Grand Harbour. Nevertheless it was sufficiently high for the Turks established there to be able to pour concentrated fire into the new fort on the tip. The fort, which is called St Elmo, and which later became the scene for one of the greatest encounters in the history of warfare, was designed by Pietro Pardo.[10] Pardo

Fort St Angelo from Dockyard creek.

37

was a Spanish engineer and he produced a fort, the design of which was severely criticized after the siege. It was made in the shape of a four-pointed star, the points of the star being the bastions which protected the curtain wall of the fort. In the re-entrant of the bastions which faced out to sea there stood a small, free-standing fortress raised higher than the main walls of St Elmo. From its ramparts flew the proud banner of the Order of the Knights of St John. On the Marsamxett side there stood a ravelin which, with its guns, was supposed to give additional fire power over the narrow stretch of water which lay between the peninsula and what is now called Tigné. As it turned out, this ravelin was a tactical error. It was captured by the Turks in the Great Siege and provided them with a secure stronghold from which to pour fire into the fort itself. Laparelli being wise after the event of its capture by the Turks castigated its designer. Laparelli pointed out that the walls of the fort had been built too high so that when they were bombarded by enemy guns their masonry collapsed and filled the ditches. If the fort had been built as a series of steps this could have been avoided. The star points of the bastions were too acute and could not be effectively covered by enfilade fire from the guns on the curtain wall. Instead, the guns had been designed to fire forward from the highest parapet and, as he pointed out, a shot fired forward can only hit one person and if it misses it is wasted. The ditch was too narrow and there was insufficient room for the defenders to assemble and carry out an effective counter-attack on the Turks. The counterscarp, which is the outer face of the ditch, was too steep and could not be effectively covered by the guns on the parapet of the fort.[11] Counter-scarps were built from material excavated from the ditch and they raised the level of the ground immediately in front of the ditch so that it could be surveyed by a soldier on the rampart without him having to lean out and expose himself.

The land front of the Isola peninsula also warranted serious consideration. Not only was it dominated by the high ground at Corradino, but it was also on the line of approach for an assaulting force attacking from the south. A star-shaped fort similar to that designed by Pardo for St Elmo was commissioned to stand back from the curtain wall on that front.[12] There remained the need to encircle the two towns of Il Borgo and Isola with strong curtain walls protected by projecting bastions where the peninsulas joined the mainland of the island. A wide ditch which ran from shore to shore pro-

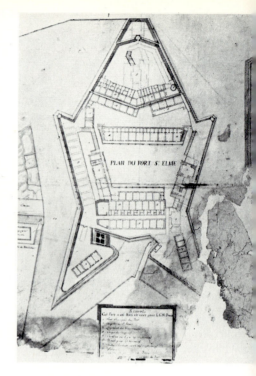

The plan of Fort St Elmo.

tected the face of the bastions which were in turn covered by the new cavaliers of St James and St John, raised up and standing well behind them. Thus we have two isolated citadels on the peninsulas which project into the Grand Harbour separated by the Dockyard creek across which was thrown a bridge of boats. The waters of the Dockyard were sealed at each end by booms, the outer one consisting of a heavy chain and the inner one a palisade of stakes driven into the bed of the creek.

There remained one outstanding problem: how to cope with the high ground on Mount Sceberras where, if Turkish forces were to capture it, heavy guns could be sited to pour devastating fire into the two towns? Time was short and money was scarce. No one was unaware of the problem, but with the urgent need to carry out a limited defence programme, the problem would have to be shelved for the time being. The new Grand Master, Jean de la Vallette, was acutely aware of the danger and nearly every day pondered its solution. The Burgomese engineer Antonio Ferramolino had been sent for by Charles V to advise the Knights and had suggested that a powerful fortress should be built on Sceberras, but the project was shelved as being too expensive. Now la Vallette called on Quinsani to discuss with him the possibility of building a new town on the Sceberras peninsula. This would be a stronger solution than an isolated fort because its defenders could be more numerous and easily victualled. It will be remembered that Bartolomeo Genga, one of the most eminent Italian military engineers, arrived in Malta early in 1558 when the study of the proposals for the new city of Valletta had already entered a decisive phase, but nothing concrete was done about the building of the new city at this stage in view of the more immediate problem of strengthening the existing fortifications around Isola and Il Borgo. There was not only the problem of building the new defences, for, in addition, time had to be left for their walls to harden before they could be brought into operation against an enemy. Freshly cut stone must be left to harden and must be left to consolidate itself on exposure to the air.

There was also the difficulty that some building work could not be done during the hot summer months. The lime mortar dries out too quickly and does not have time to grip the masonry so the lime soon powders away.

The threat of invasion hung over the island. Summer followed summer but still the axe did not fall. In the year in which it was decided to build the fort at St Elmo an abortive raid was carried out by the Turkish corsair

Dragut who was driven from Sceberras with some loss of life. Dragut moved north devastating the land and, crossing to Gozo, killed most of the men and carried the women and children into captivity. There was a feeling of expectancy, almost of desperation, in the long days of waiting as the Christian galleys thrust aggressively at the plump Turkish merchantmen, capturing them and carrying rich booty to the Knights' lair at Il Borgo.

Each Christian prize drew bursts of anger from the sultan's court in Constantinople. Stung by hurt vanity and personal loss at the capture of a vessel carrying rich possessions to the harem of the sultan, those with influential tongues clamoured for revenge against the island of Malta. And so the preparations for the grand assault began. By the autumn of 1564 the Knights knew that attack was imminent. Secret agents working in Constantinople reported that a vast invasion fleet was being fitted out. This would be the last winter of peace, for with the coming of spring and the calm seas of the Mediterranean the Turkish ships would sail, carrying the army which was to smoke out this hornets' nest. On Malta, warning beacons were erected around the coast and the open ground in front of the defences cleared of obstacles and buildings which would afford cover to the advance guards of the attacking army. Dips in the ground were levelled and humps cleared, so that lethal gunfire could be brought to bear across the no-man's land which must stretch between the opposing camps.

The Turkish intelligence system was good. For years they had watched the islands of Malta and Gozo for, even before the Knights arrived, they realized the strategic importance of Malta. A Turkish corsair, Piri Reis, who eventually became admiral to the sultan, prepared what is probably the first detailed map of Malta between about 1517 and 1521, showing the high ground upon which Mdina stands, the precipitous unscaleable cliffs of Dingli and the deep indentations of the Grand Harbour and Marsamxett, so important to sailors in search of safe anchorage.[13] Turkish agents living in the towns were sending back reports on the strength and the dispositions of the defences for, in spite of the small size of the garrison and the meagreness of the fortification, the Turks were not taking the project lightly. Since time immemorial invasions by sea have always been considered the riskiest of adventures. The Knights realized that their only hope lay in withstanding an attack for long enough to allow a relieving force to be fitted out in Sicily and come to their aid. There were some 600 members of the Order and a

The Turkish forces encamped on Mount Sceberras and surrounding the Christian army at Il Borgo and Isola. From an engraving by Perez d'Aleccio.

total defence force of about 8000 men. Against this meagre force the Turks sailed 181 men-of-war supported by numerous smaller vessels. Of the war ships 130 were galliots or galleases, swiftly rowed vessels suitable for summer seas, but needing a safe anchorage during the siege. Estimates of the size of the Turkish army vary, probably some 16,000 fighting men with supporting auxiliaries, but with a spearhead of over 6000 janissaries, the picked assault troops of the sultan reared from childhood under Spartan conditions, in whose greatest joy lay death at the service of their religion and their ruler. These men were proselytes, sons of Christian parents removed at childhood, indoctrinated, disciplined, and hardened for the bloodiest tasks in the Turkish wars.

Summer came, and on Friday, 18 May 1565, the first Turkish sail was sighted off the south of the island. It must have been an awesome sight as each ship hove up over the horizon bent on the destruction of this Christian stronghold; a sight to shake faint hearts, similar to that witnessed by the German defenders on the French coast when on that dawn in 1944 the vast allied armada emerged from the gloom, spread out across the water. Suleiman the Magnificent, architect of the assault, was 71, the greatest military leader of his day. His empire stretched from Afghanistan in the west to Aden in the south and touched the frontiers of India. His troops battered at the gates of Vienna. His suzerainty extended the length of the North African coast, and Tripoli had fallen to his guns in 1551. Now he turned his wrath upon little Malta. 'This cursed rock', he cried, 'is like a barrier interposed between us and our possessions.' Malta was the keystone of the Mediterranean and could, with its capture, become the springboard for an invasion of Sicily and Italy.

Piali Pacha was supreme admiral of the Turkish armada. He was the child of Christian parents. Found on the battlefield at Belgrade, he was saved by Suleiman and brought up in the Imperial Seraglio. He later married a niece of the sultan and was held in considerable esteem. Although his previous record seems brilliant enough, one wonders if he really deserved this position of command. He was argumentative and constantly quarrelled with Mustapha Pacha, the commander of the land forces; and, worse, he showed a lack of imagination in the handling of his magnificent fleet.

The Turkish ships made a feint landing, circled the island and eventually closed in to drop anchor in the bay of Marsaxlokk on the south of the island. The infantry and guns were disembarked and, spreading out, moved like a plague of locusts across the southern flat land of Malta. But the defenders were ready and determined to fight to the last man. Fate had thrown up for them a leader capable of matching the frenzy which the Ottoman military training might provoke.

Jean de la Valette Parisot had been born in Provence in 1494. He had a body and mind steeled in arduous warfare and a singlemindedness dedicated to the Order he now commanded. He had fought at Rhodes, had been taken a slave by the Turks and knew them well, and he possessed the three qualities necessary to inspire confidence in those he led: he was tall and dignified, calm in his manner, and resolved in his decisions.

At first, the Turkish forces lacked resolute leadership, as admiral and general fought for authority, quarrelled and criticized each other's plans. But soon the situation changed; the corsair Dragut landed with reinforcements, immediately sized up the situation, and, through the power of his personality, took control. Dragut was aggressive, perspicacious, and farsighted. Also he had the advantage of knowing his enemy. He had met and conversed with la Valette when the Knight had been a slave of the Turks. As he took over the operations for the assault Dragut summed up his inten-

Fort St Elmo with its sharp pointed bastions.

tion to win the battle. 'Till we have smoked out this nest of vipers', he cried, 'we shall do no good anywhere.'

On 24 May the heavy attack opened on the fort of St Elmo. The Turks had dragged up on to the Sceberras peninsula two 60 lb culverines, ten 80 pounders and an enormous basilisk,[14] with which they pounded the ramparts of the fort. Many of its stones had been chosen in haste and now powdered under this intense bombardment, the rubble falling forward to fill the ditches. Snipers closed to within 500 feet, picking at the heads and shoulders of those who dared to show themselves above the line of the ramparts. The little garrison of fifty-two Knights and 800 men-at-arms stood their ground. For the Turks St Elmo should have been easy meat and was expected to fall within four or five days. It formed the key to the Malta defences upon which the Turkish gunners were to wear themselves out, for until it was captured the Turkish vessels could not sail into the deep water haven of Marsamxett and lie close to the besieging army. For thirty-one days the fort stood its ground against continuous siege and heavy bombardment. Night and day there echoed up the cries of the wounded and everywhere lay the stench of death from the mangled bodies. The fierce heat of the summer sun smote the armour which encased the Knights and the smell of human flesh was overpowering. The strength of St Elmo lay in the fact that la Valette could reinforce its garrison at night, slipping fresh troops across the narrow waters of the Grand Harbour and evacuating the desperately wounded. But Dragut soon spotted this revitalizing process, redeployed his guns and sealed the sea approach to the fort. St Elmo was now a tomb – death the only answer to its defenders. Time and time again Turkish assault waves poured across the ditch only to be thrown back in confusion. At last the ravelin, which had been constructed overlooking Marsamxett harbour, was captured in a surprise attack which cost the Turks 2000 picked troops. But in spite of the losses this was a major victory, for once securely in their possession they were able to raise an artificial mound in its midst so that their snipers could pick off any of the Christian troops who exposed themselves within the walls of the fort. At dawn on 23 June the Turkish forces poured in from land and sea, the last defence crumbled and the Ottoman flag ran up to the masthead. What should have been a speedy, simple operation cost the Turks some 8000 dead including their leader, Dragut. On 18 June he had been struck and mortally wounded by a shot from the cannon on Fort St

Angelo. His condition had been kept secret from the troops, but now his death could no longer be concealed and a wave of depression ran through the Turkish army. It was with no feeling of elation that Mustapha Pacha surveyed the ruins of St Elmo and turned his attention upon two citadels of Il Borgo and Isola. 'If so small a son has cost us so dear, what price shall we have to pay for so large a father.' How right he was! In the days that followed reverses heaped their calumny upon the Turkish attackers. Acting on false intelligence imparted by a deceiving informer they attacked the land front of Il Borgo defended by the Castillian Knights, and what should have

Aleccio's depiction of the Turkish assault on Fort St Elmo.

Plan of Malta made in Rome in 1565, showing the Turkish investment of Il Borgo and Isola. It also shows, probably inaccurately, the lines of a Turkish fortress constructed on Mount Sceberras, the peninsula at the top of the drawing.

been the weak point turned out to be the most impregnable bastion of the defence. Their guns battered at the exposed face of the bastion of Castille and their engineers ran forward to construct a high wooden tower from which they hoped to dominate the defenders. But the defenders trumped their ace. From a concealed gun position at the base of the bastion the Knights threw out a volley of chain shot which severed the supports of the high wooden tower, bringing it and its unfortunate occupants crashing to the ground.

A fresh Turkish attack developed on Isola and Turkish engineers rolled forward a time bomb designed to explode on the parapet of the Fort St Michael. However, the time delay was too long and some brave Knights were able to roll it back into the Turkish lines before it had time to explode. But the pressure of the attack on Fort St Michael seemed overpowering. The Knights were giving valuable ground foot by foot and, with no reinforcements close enough to give relief, it looked as if the battle in that quarter was lost and success within the grasp of Mustapha. At this eleventh hour, by one of the ironies of war, hurried word was brought to the Turkish general that a relieving force had landed from Sicily and was attacking the supply train of the Turkish army. With reluctance and exasperation, Mustapha ordered the retreat, swinging his forces in a circle and facing the threat from the Marsa. Too late the truth was learned that it was only a contingent of cavalry which had sallied out from Mdina, cutting to pieces the undefended supply train and killing the wounded in their tents. It must have been a bitter pill for Mustapha Pacha, who had been advised by some of his counsellors to attack and capture Mdina at an early stage in the war before mounting the main assault on Fort St Elmo. Clearly all was not well within the Turkish army. The repulse of repeated attacks was eating into the morale of its troops. Dysentery and fever had broken out on a large scale, possibly the result of drinking water from the wells on the Marsa which had been poisoned by the Knights when the Turks first landed. Time was running out; August was moving fast into September and Piali feared for the safety of his fleet. With September would come the sudden storms which would imperil the security of the galleys at sea. Two alternatives lay open to him. On the one hand, he could abandon the infantry to a winter siege on Malta, withdrawing the fleet to the safety of Constantinople but thereby exposing the army to the possibility of an attack from Sicily only sixty miles to the north, and leaving it with no means of evacuation. The other course lay in the complete abandonment of the siege and an ignominious withdrawal to Turkey. Few Turkish commanders would have had the courage to report such a major defeat to the passionate ruler of the Ottoman empire. In this state of uncertainty the bombardment of the defences continued and Mustapha Pacha resolved to sweep clean the remaining pocket of resistance in Mdina in case he were forced to winter on the island. The capture of the old town would at least provide winter quarters. A diversionary attack was mounted and Turkish troops moved forward for the assault, believing that at last they had an easy prey. But the garrison commander of Mdina was a wily man. He summoned all the Maltese men and women within the citadel, dressed them in an assortment of uniforms and paraded them in strength along the ramparts of the city. The Turks were so dispirited at this apparent demonstration of strength on the high walls of the hill fortress that they withdrew in dismay.

The Grand Master had sent repeated requests to the Viceroy of Sicily for relief to raise the siege, but for several reasons the Viceroy had not acted promptly. He rightly gauged the need for a well-organized relieving force adequate to do its job effectively. But he must have feared that should this force be lost at sea or decimated in a fruitless attempt to relieve Malta his own flank would be opened and his main task, the defence of Sicily, prejudiced before he faced the blow he must expect to receive should the Knights' island stronghold fall. Slowly the build-up of forces in Sicily went ahead. That year the gales came early and it was not until 7 September that the relief force approached the undefended north of the island and put ashore some 10,000 men. Admittedly this seems a small force, but sufficient in view of the low Turkish morale inflicted by disease and continual reversal in the face of the Knights' defences. Once again, Admiral Piali showed his lack of resolution. His ships outnumbered the relieving ships by about three to one and yet he made no attempt to drive into them and sink them at sea, nor indeed to harass them during the hazardous hours occupied by the disembarking of the troops. The Sicilian troops moved south and quartered for the night on the high ground near Mdina. The Turkish general received the information and started to withdraw his forces with rapidity before they could be attacked by these fresh troops itching for battle. Only when most of his forces had been evacuated to the ships did Mustapha learn the full story of the smallness of the relieving force. Perhaps to save face, he relanded 9000 reluctant Turkish soldiers and turned to face the Sicilians, but the ensuing battle was an unequal one. The fresh Christian soldiers, thirsting to avenge their beleaguered cousins, burst upon the small Turkish force which fled in disorder to the sea and to its ships. By the evening of 8 September it was all over. The siege had lasted three and a half months. Everywhere lay desolation. Il Borgo and Isola were shattered and not one single house remained undamaged. Gaping holes were torn in all the defensive walls and rubble filled the ditches. The ground was pitted with shot and mine and channelled with tunnels, some of which had already collapsed while others were in imminent danger of doing so. It was a scene of desolation which must have dismayed the most stouthearted, for everyone was aware that the Turks were not in the habit of giving up and that one day they would return to complete their task. But as it turned out it was the last great attempt of the Ottoman empire to break into the western Mediterranean. The siege in Malta had cast doubt on the efficiency of the Turkish military machine. The assault army had been proved vulnerable to the determination of a well-placed and resolute defender. Six years after the repulse of the Turkish army from Malta, at the Battle of Lepanto, the proud Turkish fleet was finally brought to action. On 7 October 1571, within the confined waters which lay between the island of Morea and the mainland of Greece, not far south east of the heel of Italy, there gathered the greatest assembly of battle fleets the modern world had known and they fought the last great battle between oar-driven ships. Defeat once and for all destroyed the Turkish chance of converting the Mediterranean into a Turkish lake. The Turkish admiral, Ali Pasha, confident, though showing the weakness of resolution which had characterized Turkish fleet action off Malta, led the central squadron and commanded the Turkish flagship. As the weight of allied armour and fire power poured in upon his ship and wave upon wave of Don John's infantry clambered onto his deck, wounded in the head, he pleaded in vain for his life. But a Spanish pikeman hacked off his head and spiking it on to his long weapon waved it aloft to the final disconsolation of the Ottoman forces. It was a turning point in history.

A spate of books followed the relief of the great siege of Malta. Two were written by men who were present during the battle, Francisco Balbi de Correggio and Antoine Cressin.[15] Antonio Francesco Cirni came with the relieving force from Sicily and collected valuable information from the survivors of the siege. Most of the other accounts are based on these episodes and vary in their accuracy. The valour of the defenders and the raising of the siege was afforded such acclaim throughout Western Europe that the standing of the Knights of St John and their Maltese comrades at arms stood high in the estimation of the princes of Europe. Several of the military treatises which followed refer to the battle and draw valuable conclusions. Vincenzo Scamozzi, one of the greatest architects and military engineers of his day in Italy, wrote about Malta in 1615: 'Small islands such as Corfu and others, will be secure if their fortifications are constructed in this manner [referring to his recommendations] because when an enemy is present he will always be inconvenienced by lack of food, water, wood, hay, straw, and many other things – this is how the island of Malta defended itself valorously against the Turks.'[16]

[1] Fedden (Robin) and Thompson (John). *Crusader Castles* (London 1950), page 27, and see also Rey (G.) *Étude sur les monuments de l'architecture militaire des Croisés en Syrie* (Paris 1871).

[2] Landström (Björn). *The Ship* (London 1961), pages 127–41.

[3] O'Neil (B. H. St J.) 'Rhodes and the Origin of the Bastion', *Antiquaries Journal*, Vol 34 (January–April 1954), pages 44–5.

[4] *The Codex of Francesco Laparelli da Cortona, written in Malta 1566–1567*, 26.

[5] Bonello (Vincenzo). 'Il primo architetto dell'Ordine a Malta' in *Malta Missjimarja* (April 1952).

[6] Liber Bullarum. A.O.M. 419, ff. ccxii–iii, letter dated 1543.

[7] For further information see Zahra (Lawrence). *Vittoriosa – The city of the Great Siege* (Malta 1965), and a series of studies on the ramparts of Vittoriosa in the *Sunday Times of Malta* (4 September, 11 September, 18 September, 25 September 1966).

[8] See also Zahra (Lawrence). 'Fort S. Angelo, Sentinel of the Grand Harbour' in the *Sunday Times of Malta* (28 March 1965).

[9] Perez (Matteo d'Aleccio). *The true depiction of the investment and attack suffered by the Island of Malta at the hands of the Turks in the year of Our Lord 1565* (Bologna 1631). Translated with notes by Commander D. J. Calnan (Malta 1965).

[10] Vincenzo Bonello has suggested that Pardo is really Pietro da Prato, an engineer who came from Prato in Tuscany.

[11] Laparelli *Codex. The defects of S. Elmo*. 38B.

[12] There is some uncertainty about what sort of fort was built at S. Michael to cover the land face of Isola (Senglea). In my book on *The Building of Malta*, p.21, I refer to a star-shaped fort, similar to S. Elmo, having been built to the designs of Pedro Pardo and some early engravings of the Great Siege actually show this. However, Perez d'Aleccio's frescoes, the most reliable source, show a cavalier similar to those constructed on the land front of Il Borgo. Certainly, at some time or other, a square fort with embrasures on three sides and an open parapet on the front stood on this site. It was demolished in 1927 to make way for a school, but a model and drawings have survived.

[13] Vadala (M. Agius). 'The first map of Malta – drawn by a Turkish corsair', *Sunday Times of Malta* (24 October, 31 October, 7 November 1965).

[14] A large brass cannon capable of throwing heavy shot.

[15] Balbi (Francisco di Correggio). *La Verdadera Relacion de todo lo que este año de MDLXV ha sucedido en la Isla de Malta, ecc.* (Barcelona 1565), translated by Balbi (Henry Alexander) (Copenhagen 1961). Bradford (Ernle). *The Siege of Malta 1565* (London 1965).
Cressin (Antoine). *Vray discours de la guerre et siege de Malte par les Turcs* (Paris 1565).
Other important descriptions include –
Curione (Celio Secondo). *A new history of the war in Malta, 1565*, translated by Granville (Alex. Pacha) (Rome 1928).
Castellani (Vincenzo). *De Bello Melitensi Historia* (Pesaro 1566).
Vesperano (Antonio). *De Bello Melitensi* (Perugia 1566).
See also Galea (Joseph). 'The Siege and its writers', *Sunday Times of Malta* (5 September 1965).

[16] *Dell'idea della architettura universale di Vincenzo Scamozzi, architetto Veneto*, Venice 1615, Part I, Lib II, Cap. XXLL, P.181.

Chapter 3: A City is Born

The guns were silent and all round lay the ruins on that little rock of limestone 400 years ago. The defenders of Malta had been hammered for nearly four months by picked troops from the finest armada ever assembled by the Turkish sultan. The siege had been lifted and the Crusader Knights of St John decided to take an irrevocable step and stand firm against all future threats. For nearly three centuries they had fought a rearguard action from the Holy Land, first to Cyprus, then to Rhodes, and finally in 1530 to Malta. This far they would withdraw, but no farther. The decision was not taken without great heart searching and many Knights dissented, preferring the greater safety of the mainland. It was largely due to the persuasion of one man, Francesco Laparelli, that the doubters and the faint-hearted did not carry the day. Laparelli, lean, hard, with gaunt cavernous cheeks and penetrating eyes, was a man of action. Steeled in the Italian wars, he had become one of the foremost exponents of the art of military fortification under the guidance of Serbelloni at Cortona. After working on Michelangelo's defences he was chosen for Malta by the Pope as a man of determination. He sailed from Italy and arrived in the last days of the year 1565 when the dust of war had barely settled.

The significance of his visit lies in the fact that he proposed and carried out the erection of a new planned city on a virgin site. A city with a difference. It did not grow up in the amorphous way in which most cities develop; it was created as a completely new town and Laparelli claimed, perhaps not with complete accuracy, that this was the first occasion when a city was built where previously nothing had existed. 'From the time of Cain's Enoch city', he wrote, 'until now, no one has tried to begin a completely new city. Where people have begun to build a new city there has always been something existing – there has always been some habitation. For example, Alexandria was made by Alexander, but it is impossible that there was not already a village there because it was an important commercial site. But this city on the mountain is really new.'

We now know better. There were many Roman cities constructed on virgin sites, and, in the twelfth and thirteenth centuries, the warring kings of France and England built for themselves bastide towns like Aigues Mortes and Caernarvon; their street pattern and fortified walls followed a grid plan and a regular layout deep in the heart of enemy-occupied country. Laparelli's city, however, is unique because we still have a written record of the trials and tribulations which beset its designer from the day when he first put forward his proposal to his departure from the island four years later. Laparelli kept most of his reports[1] and these have been handed down to our own day. They provide a unique record of one of the most important planned towns of the Renaissance.

Malta had successfully withstood a prolonged siege in the previous year and had emerged a battered haulk, but still the acknowledged hingepin in the southern defence of Christianity. She was the cork in the bottle of the western Mediterranean, which if drawn would allow the waters of Islamic invasion to surge into the Christian lands of the West. It had been a battle fought with all the fierce fanaticism associated with religious wars at a time when an iron curtain was drawn across the map of Europe dividing it into two camps more irreconcilable than those today. This was not one of the polite, white-gloved battles of the condottiere of the Italian peninsula, with its manoeuvre and counter-manoeuvre the vanquished accepting defeat with the equanimity of losing at chess, neither side entertaining the idea of fighting to the death or unconditional surrender. The siege of Malta was a bloody fight with quarter neither sought nor granted. On a long tongue of land whose prominence commanded the defences of the Knights, the Turkish batteries first pounded the little fort of St Elmo for eighteen days with a continuous cannonade. Her garrison fought to the last man, her ramparts broken 'even down to the sheer rock on which the fort had been erected'. The Turkish batteries then swung in an arc to menace Il Borgo, the main stronghold of the Knights, and only the timely arrival of a relieving force from Sicily and the

Portrait of Francesco Laparelli.

ravages of an epidemic in the Turkish camp forced them to abandon the siege and withdraw to Turkey.

However, many of the defenders were dispirited, their guns were shattered and their ammunition supplies low. They felt that this was no more than a respite and the opportunity should be taken to evacuate the island and remove the defending force to the mainland of Italy. From their experience in Rhodes they were convinced of the truth of the axiom 'The Turk always returns'.

There was a body of dissatisfied Knights led by a 72-year-old vacillating Grand Master, who had borne the full responsibility of withstanding the siege. It was into this atmosphere that Laparelli was precipitated on his arrival on the island. He sensed the urgency of the occasion and within six days he submitted his first report on the idea of building a completely new city on the high tongue of land which had dominated the old defences of the Knights. On 3 January 1566 he reported the main outlines of his fortified city to the Grand Master la Valette. Laparelli's prognosis was so accurate and his proposal so sound that the fortifications of Valletta today still broadly follow the delineation he was able to sketch out in a mere six days. With astute argument he played on the susceptibilities of the uncommitted Knights. In spite of intelligence reports, the Turks would not, he thought, return immediately to the attack. They were refitting their armada mainly to save face and in order to frighten the defenders of Malta. It would be shameful to leave the island without putting up a fight as everyone knew that Malta was a shield for the whole of Christianity. In the first stage Laparelli called for 3000 sappers to work for three months, supported by a defending force of 3000 troops. A further force of 1000 sappers would be needed to work for another month in concealed positions should a new attack develop. All available timber should immediately be brought over from the old town to the new site and committed to the work; then, the Rubicon having been crossed, there would be no turning back. The children should be evacuated from the island at least until the autumn so as to save food and protect them. Laparelli argued that if the Knights were to evacuate the island it would cost as much to destroy the old fortifications as it would now cost to build new ones, and they could hardly leave the remnants of a fortified island to the Turks.

Although many wanted to leave Malta and most of the precious possessions were ready packed for transit to Sicily, there was a body of opinion which favoured the rebuilding of the old town of Il Borgo and the castle of St Angelo, for, it was argued, they had already withstood one siege from this position and could do so again. Laparelli was sceptical, pointing out that it would cost at least as much to rebuild the old fortifications and these would still be overlooked from the higher ground on the tongue of land where he now proposed to build his fortified city.

Ten days later he was again impatiently reporting to the Grand Master that they had already lost fifteen days, had not got hold of any sappers and still had made no decision. Every day delayed was a day nearer the time when the Turkish armada would return. Nevertheless by 30 January, nearly a month after Laparelli's first design had been submitted, many had accepted in broad principle the idea of moving to a new site.

Several other notable military engineers had been called upon for their advice. Scipione Campi from Pesaro was in Malta when the Turkish attack developed. He survived the siege and was able to make suggestions to Laparelli for the improvement of his city plan.

Lanci, who visited Malta before the siege, must have returned after it, for, in Laparelli's Codex, there is a 'copy of a memo left by Baldassare Lanci of Urbino about fortifications and the new city on the island of Malta', in which he talks of the great destruction which has been wrought on the fortifications and the remedial work necessary to repair the damage. Lanci refers to a design and a model he has made although it is not clear whether this is the design he made before the siege or one produced afterwards. 'I have studied St Elmo', he noted, 'and this is the best place to make an impregnable city. It is more healthy than Il Borgo and is higher with cool breezes. The new city will be surrounded by water and guarded by two hundred canne of land.[2] There is deep water round it. It can be guarded by few people and the site is big enough to hold the whole population of the island and, if necessary, all its animals. I have made a design and a measured model, and placed on the model the trace of the fortifications, roads, squares, the division of the houses, palaces, churches, hospitals, and other places which it will be necessary to build.'

From the memo it is clear that Lanci's proposals were detailed and thorough. He claims to have measured the site and taken levels, to have built a sample of the wall for all to see. He seems also to have taken off quantities and determined the cost of the work. Although in retrospect we may doubt

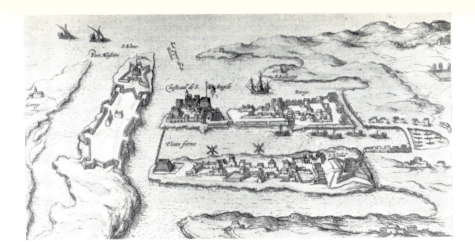

Braun & Hohenberg's drawing of Valletta, Il Borgo and Isola from *Civitates Orbis Terrarum* (1572–) probably shows Lanci's intentions for the new city.

the accuracy of his calculations, Lanci seemed confident at the time that he could give an accurate figure and he even quoted a system operative in Ancient Rome. In that city, he said, architects projecting a design had to state how much it would cost, and if it was necessary to spend more than they had estimated the architects would have to pay the balance out of their own pockets. If they had not sufficient money to pay they received severe punishment.

Lanci's city was to be encircled by a fifty-foot road which would serve the fortification. The main road of the city would run from the city gate in a large platform or square behind the front line, which was to stretch across the peninsula over the spine of the hill, to a central square and on to Fort St Elmo. This road would be forty-five feet wide and the other roads of the city would be twenty feet wide.

Lanci's main square was to be 230 feet square and around it would be disposed the palace of the Grand Master, the church, and other important public buildings.

Laparelli's strongest support came from Gabrio Serbelloni, of Milan. He and Laparelli had known each other at Cortona in the war against Siena. Of noble family and a cousin of Pius IV, Serbelloni had enlisted as a Knight of Malta in his youth. In the year 1566 when he visited Malta to advise on the new city he was 57 years old, a veteran of many campaigns, military engineer to the King of Spain, town planning expert in Rome, and a respected counsellor to the Knights. The Maltese historian Bosio says that Serbelloni arrived on the island in March 1566 and was consulted on Laparelli's plan for the new city. He gave his wholehearted recommendation and wrote to both the Pope and the King of Spain singing its praises.

On 14 March Serbelloni sailed for Messina in a galley of the Order where he met Don Garzia, Viceroy of Sicily, and was instrumental in bringing about a reconciliation between Don Garzia and the Grand Master of Malta, the former promising to send immediate aid in the form of money, men, and materials in order to help build the new city. Serbelloni returned to Italy and, joining the fleet which had been fitted out by the Pope, sailed and took part in the famous battle of Lepanto in 1571 which once and for all crushed the power of the Turkish navy. It was largely due to Serbelloni's valiant efforts in rallying vacillating allies that such a resounding victory was won by the allied fleet. The arguments in Malta now revolved around the extent of the city and the exact line on the peninsula across which the narrow landward defences should be constructed.

Throughout the Italian Renaissance many architects had been pre-occupied with the design of ideal cities and most had regarded them as exercises in three dimensional space, laid out in a geometrical pattern usually with strict symmetry. The architectural literature of the fifteenth and sixteenth centuries in Italy is filled with proposals for ideal planned cities. Much of Alberti's large treatise on building[3] is concerned with town planning, from the choice of a suitable site to the detailed designs of house elevations. There can be little doubt that Laparelli was aware of Alberti's work, if not at first hand, certainly in the town-building ideas which had been absorbed into day-to-day practice. Both Alberti and Vitruvius, the only ancient architectural writer whose books have been preserved for the modern world, conceived of a city as a complete work of art to which individual buildings were related.

Antonio Averlino, called Il Filarete, was probably the first architect to design a city enclosed within a circle, a shape particularly dear to the hearts of fifteenth-century Neo-Platonists because it was thought to be the most perfect shape in nature.[4] Filarete's proposals for an ideal city to be built in the north of Italy were never realized and his book remained in manuscript.[5] His city, Sforzinda, consisted of sixteen main roads radiating from a central square, embraced by a ring road and terminated by obtuse-angled bastions whose points touch a circular ditch.

From the time of Filarete many of the proposals put forward by Italian military engineers consisted of a centrally planned city enclosed within a fortified wall of bastions whose extremities were designed to fall upon the circumference of a circle. Within this fortified embrace the road pattern was either radial or grid-iron so that the whole city became symmetrical about its central square. Many projects died on the drawing board, but some survived.

Vitry-le-François was designed by Girolamo Marini and built in 1545; Palmanova, in the Republic of Venice, was constructed between 1566 and 1593; Zamosc near Lublin, by Bernardo Morando of Padua, in 1578; Coeworden in Holland in 1583; and there were others.

Pietro Cataneo's *I quattro primi libri di architettura* was published by the Aldine press of Venice in 1554, just twelve years before Laparelli undertook the task of building a new city in Malta. The first, and by far the longest, of Cataneo's books is devoted to the design of new cities, eight of which are illustrated, two being for construction on the coast. All Cataneo's cities have a grid-iron layout of streets, a central square with regularly disposed smaller squares, and a large assembly ground in front of the citadel. It seems certain that both Alberti's and Cataneo's treatises were known to Laparelli during his employment in the Vatican.

It would be strange if he were not aware of the town-planning projects being undertaken in his Spanish American colonies by the Spanish king, who had close ties with the Knights. The new town of Puebla de los Angeles with its grid-iron plan had been founded in 1531, the year after the gift of Malta by Charles V to the Knights of St John. The ideas on city planning crystallizing in Spain were published in the form of royal ordinances on 3 July 1573,[6] and many of them stem directly from Alberti, showing how widespread had become the Italian's ideas: the zoning of noxious trades, the proportions of the main and secondary squares, the orientation of buildings, uniformity of house designs so as to make the town beautiful, and the need to depend on a fruitful countryside to maintain the townspeople. However, the most interesting instruction in our context is that which requires the settlers to select a vacant site which may be taken without harming the interests of the natives, or with their consent.

Laparelli's proposals were to be different. Undoubtedly some of these Italian solutions were known to the Knights who were drawn from the most noble families of Europe. Laparelli therefore had to contend with counter-suggestions of lay opinion. But these suggestions he dismissed as being unsuitable to the site which, because of the undulating terrain, could not accommodate a text-book solution.

The foundation stone of the new city was laid amid great pomp and circumstance and the site christened Valletta in honour of the Grand Master who had led his Knights to victory against the Turkish armada. Laparelli recorded this event in his diary. 'On 28th March 1566 began the New City on the island of Malta. It is begun on the hill which is isolated except from one side and has all these good qualities which we have always stated. The land front is formed at a distance of five hundred canne from Fort St Elmo. There is no habitation, ancient or modern, on that hill. (I think no city has been founded where there was no habitation.) St Spirito Mass has been sung under a canopy planted near the position of the front line. After singing the Mass, Father spoke. After the sermon a procession sang the

The high rock walls of Valletta's fortifications—St Michael's demi-bastion.

St Michael's counterguard – a sentrybox on Laparelli's land front of Valletta.

Litany, another oration saying the name of the new city, which is Valletta, and passed towards the middle of the front where the main gate must be put and called the gate of St George. Then it passed to the four bulwarks. After this the foundation stone was laid, sculptured with the Holy Cross of the Order with its eight angles. And the Grand Master gave me a chain of gold.'

The foundation stone contained the inscription in Latin – 'Fra Jean De La Vallette, Grand Master of the Hospitaller Order of Jerusalem, mindful of the danger of which, a year before, his Knights and the Maltese people were exposed during the siege by the Turks, having consulted the heads of the Order about the construction of a new city and the fortifying of the same by walls, ramparts, and towers sufficient to resist any attack or to repel or, at least, to withstand the Turkish enemy, on Thursday the 28th March 1566,[7] after the invocation of the Almighty God, of the Virgin Mother, of the Patron Saint John the Baptist, and of the other Saints, to grant that the work commenced should lead to the prosperity and the happiness of the whole Christian community, and to the advantage of the Order, laid the foundation stone of the City on the hill called Sceberras by the natives, and having granted for its arms a golden lion on a red shield wished it to be called by his name, Valletta.'

Work progressed slowly, for it was an arduous job requiring excavations in the solid rock and everything had to be imported to this virgin site. Laparelli grew impatient and offered to return to Italy to recruit labour. However, he made it clear that inducements would be necessary to compete in what was already a difficult market. The terms of contract make interesting reading and these conditions of employment, made 400 years ago, seem strangely modern. The workmen were to be paid a daily rate from the day they signed up in Italy, irrespective of whether they worked or not. They were to be transported to Malta free and given free rations while at sea. For each day they worked they were to receive a bonus, and should work be stopped because of bad weather they were to be paid a bonus for the amount of work they had carried out. If a workman became ill he would receive his basic pay packet, but without the bonus, and he was to receive free medical care in the hospital of the Order of St John. Lodgings were to be available close to the site and rations were to be provided for which the workmen would pay, on the understanding that these would not be too expensive.

Alternatively they should be permitted to purchase their own wine, meat, and other foods which must be made available for them. They were to receive full pay on feast days when work stopped and, when no longer needed, should be provided with a free passage back to one of three specified ports in Italy. Finally, clear differentials were established for the various grades of foremen and overseers. Laparelli was also prepared to recruit bombardiers and their assistants. Before being taken on these men would be given the usual tests. They would be required to clean the gun, put powder in it, followed by the wad and the cannon ball, pressing it home with the rod. They would cool the piece and lay the gun, carrying out the master's instructions.

We have a clear description of the sort of city Laparelli envisaged. There were, he said, three places where the front line could be drawn across the peninsula. Firstly, on a line at a distance 300 canne from Fort St Elmo. This would have placed the fortification half way between the present site of the Grand Master's palace and St John's church where the peninsula is narrowest. Secondly, at 500 canne from the gate of St Elmo, a line most strongly favoured by Laparelli and the one finally constructed. The present city gate is 500 canne from St Elmo. And thirdly, at 800 canne, in what is now Floriana, roughly running through the present site of St Publius's church. Although this front line would have commanded the heights of Corradino and was near to the water hole on the Marsa, Laparelli disapproved pointing out that it would enclose an area too large for the city and might leave a vulnerable gap between the end of the city and Fort St Elmo.

Although he prepared designs for both of the first two solutions[8] Laparelli soon concentrated on the second proposal maintaining that here was a site which 'if there are victuals and munitions, will be impregnable'. Consequently he urged the Knights to begin with 'a spirit of iron to close the city until it embraces St Elmo'.

If it appears there will be no time to do this, the Order should construct a powerful fort behind the 500 canne line making it impossible for the Turks to land on the peninsula and establish themselves. The distance between the two forts would be about 660 yards which could be commanded by the guns on the forts. Three thousand troops would be needed to man these forts supported by sixty pieces of artillery trained to fire along fixed lines, and 100 arquebuses, or portable guns. The front line would be comparatively safe from attack as it overlooked lower ground in front.

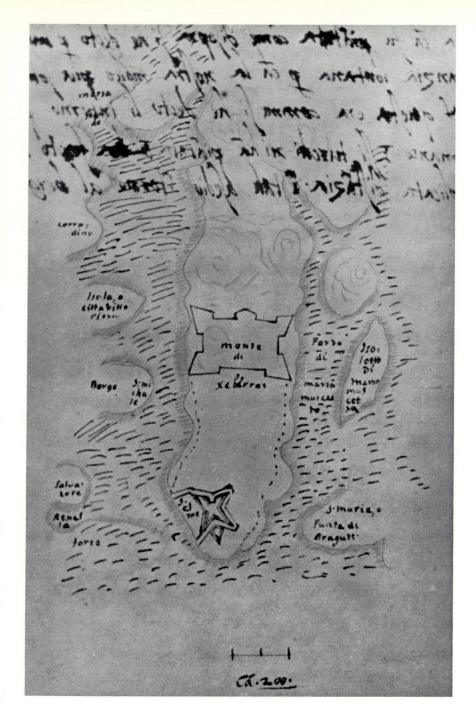

Laparelli's suggested fortifications.

Map showing the relation of the new city of Valletta to the peninsulas of Il Borgo and Isola, made by Lafrery in 1566.

Laparelli reckoned the fortifications of the new city would cost some 345,000 man-days to build, and this was cheaper than demolishing all existing defences of Malta and evacuating the island which would require some 480,000 man-working days. However, he was careful to add a note of warning that it was impossible to give an accurate estimate because of the nature of the site. Those who thought this possible, and here he must have been thinking of Baldassare Lanci, were misguided. As things turned out, Laparelli's estimate was wide of the mark. In the first instance he called for a labour force of 3000 sappers for four months, but in June 1567, seventeen months after his first report, he still needed 4000 sappers to work until May 1568. Laparelli's fortifications were built according to his plan which was illustrated in Antonio Lafrery's *Tavole geografiche* of 1566. This shows a complete enceinte of wall from Fort St Elmo, which lies askew the site, to the land front on the 500 canne line. The land front is braced by four bastions designed with obtuse angles and fairly blunt points, which were less likely to be knocked off by enemy gun fire than the earlier sharp pointed bastions of Fort St Elmo. Between the four bastions, and covered by enfilade fire from their flanks, lay three lengths of curtain wall, the central one pierced by the city gate of St George. Dry ditches lay in front of the bastions sufficiently wide to allow a raiding party to assemble in them and break out of the city. The controversy as to whether fortified ditches should be dry or filled with water had raged for a long time. 'Water is good – it stops a sudden attack', wrote Laparelli. 'It is especially good against a surprise attack and is useful for small forts manned by few men, they can keep fish in ditches. But a dry ditch is better for a large fort defended by many soldiers because it allows a force to sally out, and once out their line of retreat cannot be easily cut.' He pointed out that it was easier to clean out a dry ditch if part of the escarpment had fallen in, a point noticed by Alberti 100 years earlier.[9] If the enemy threw twigs or fascines into a dry ditch they could be set on fire, but in a wet ditch these formed a staircase across which the enemy could pass, and if, of course, the water in a ditch froze, an unlikely event in Malta, the ditch became a bridge for the attackers. The bastions were to be low, some eight feet thick and some sixteen feet high to the string course and they should be constructed of earth. The Knights should construct stone bastions only when they knew that there would be time for the wall to harden and the stone consolidate itself on exposure to the air.

Under gunfire a new stone wall would crack in shape like a spider's web and when the wall crumbled it would fill the ditch. However, in May 1567 Laparelli called for more impressive fortifications in stone. The escarpment was to be sixty feet from the string course to the bottom of the ditch, the excavated material being used to fill any ditches outside the counterscarp so that the attackers would be exposed. The guns were to have positions constructed on the flanks of the bastions forty-eight feet wide on the face increasing to fifty-six feet at the rear to allow them to traverse and the platforms were to be twenty-four feet deep to accommodate the recoil. Behind the bastions nine cavaliers were to be built, of which two were actually constructed. Laparelli marked the positions of the remaining seven so that the sites could be left vacant and no buildings built upon them. Cavaliers are raised forts placed behind the bastions, high enough for their guns to dominate the surrounding countryside and cover any enemy attempt to break through the bastions. They had the advantage that should their walls be shattered by long range enemy fire, the masonry could not fall into the ditches and provide a pathway for the advancing infantry. Within the city itself walls were to be dug and the ditch in front of Fort St Elmo, no longer needed for defence, filled with water. Windmills to grind corn were to be constructed in sheltered positions protected from the view of the enemy.

On the northern shore of the city, in Marsamxett harbour, a haven was to be built for the galleys of the Order. This, called the Manderaggio, was begun, stone being used to construct the houses in the city, but was never completed, partly because the masons ran into a hard stratum which was unsuitable for building. The Manderaggio is shown as an oval creek in Lafrery's drawing of the city.

The form of the city came last, after the defensive ring had been finalized. It is not even shown on the Lafrery drawing but we know it was submitted to la Valette before the foundation stone was laid in March 1566. Laparelli's proposals for this part of the scheme are perhaps its most interesting aspect for us today for, whereas our ideas on defence have had to be radically rethought, our conception of a city street plan still bears recognizable resemblance to the theories held four centuries ago. Art historians are prone to accept those passages in source material which fit their theories and lay aside those uncomfortable quotations which do not. A whole theory of classical art and architecture has been built upon the writings of the Neo-Platon-

Lafrery's drawing for the new city of Valletta.

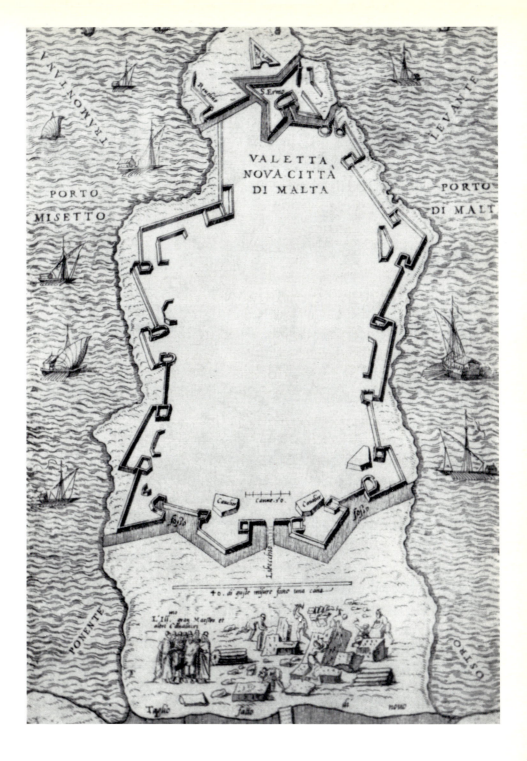

ists of the fifteenth century in Italy. It is based on the belief that beauty is to be found in certain geometrical shapes having an inherent quality which if altered is shattered. 'I shall define Beauty', wrote Alberti, 'to be a harmony of all the parts, in whatsoever subject it appears, fitted together with such proportion and connection, that nothing could be added, diminished or altered, but for the worse.'[10] In line with this thought Renaissance architects tended to design cities, 'for a city, according to the opinion of philosophers, be no more than a great house',[11] on a geometrical pattern, enscribed within a geometrical form with their roads either radiating from the centre or disposed to form by their crossing a series of rectangular plots.

The disturbing passage occurs in Book IV, chapter V, of Alberti. 'If the city is noble and powerful', he wrote, 'the streets should be straight and broad, which carries an air of greatness and majesty; but if it is only a small town or a fortification, it will be better, and as safe, not for the streets to run straight to the gates; but to have them wind about sometimes to the right, sometimes to the left, near the wall, and especially under the towers upon the wall; and within the heart of the town, *it will be handsomer not to have them straight*[12] but winding about several ways, backwards and forwards like the course of a river. For this, besides that by appearing so much the longer, they will *add to the idea of the greatness of the town,* they will likewise conduce very much to beauty and convenience, and be a greater security against all accidents and emergencies.' Undoubtedly Alberti was borrowing from Aristotle's statement in the *Politics* that winding streets are better for defence but straight streets are more beautiful. But Alberti changes ground and suggests that on occasions winding streets are more handsome than straight ones. This cuts right across the generally held belief that Renaissance architecture is an art of straight lines and circles, the flowing curve not being introduced until the Baroque. Who ever saw an Italian Renaissance house with winding walls?

A recent author[13] has suggested that this may be a hangover from mediaeval principles of town design, maintaining that what we now often think of as an undisciplined arrangement of streets, all higgledy-piggledy, in old cities was, in fact, a carefully adjusted disposition to obtain the best townscape effects for a pedestrian passing through their streets – a mediaeval theory of the picturesque. Camillo Sitte, writing in the nineteenth century, was convinced that much of the apparently picturesque muddle of Italian towns was far from accidental. De Wolfe quotes Sabbionetta, near Mantua, built between 1550 and 1564 by Vespasian Gonsaga. Although this *new town* does not have winding streets, it certainly does not fit into the accepted pattern of Renaissance planning. It is not a grid-iron plan and its squares and public buildings are not symmetrically disposed. Let us now turn to Laparelli's original proposals for Valletta. 'Many writers', he said, 'praise the central form for a city with many angles [This is the radial plan formed like a spoked wheel], but I have found from experience that it is good to follow the lines of the site and not to try to force nature into regular lines. So we shall make a form which is suggested by the site itself, and it seems to me that this should be done everywhere. I shall arrange the streets differently from what many are thinking.' Then, inspired by Alberti, he goes on, 'I shall make for beauty only one large street in the middle of the city, the others being narrow and with a *pleasant and sweet serpentine way*, and this I shall do because only a city in humid climates should have wide streets so that the wind and the sun can take away the humidity. Narrow streets are cooler because they are not dominated by the sun. For a windy place like Malta it is necessary to find a way to break the wind with trees or high walls, but this cannot happen here because all the island (and especially this site) is bare and without trees. So it will help to make the streets serpentine like Pisa, which *is fine to see* and certainly was made in this way to break the strength of the winds. People should plant trees around the walls which will be useful in peacetime, and in wartime wood is one of the most important munitions. Trees which grow quickly should be planted.'

In the construction of Valletta the serpentine streets were replaced by straight ones, perhaps because of the problem of allocating strangely shaped sites for housing, possibly due to the prejudice of the Council of the Order which for centuries had been trained with military precision to rationalize a site, or even because many felt that the grid-iron plan, which was to hold with a grip of iron the minds of Beaux-Arts planners for centuries to come, was the thing to follow.

No drawing remains of Laparelli's design, but we have some indication of the way in which he proposed to distribute the streets and public buildings in a report entitled 'Estimate of the sizes of units in the New City' supposedly written in mid 1566. There was to be one main street thirty-three feet wide running the full 1080 yards from Fort St Elmo to the new city gate.

This street was to have on each side two serpentine streets, twenty-three feet wide, and of the same length as the main street.

There were to be eight serpentine crossing streets, each about twenty feet wide and 540 yards long. With a grid-iron pattern these streets would certainly not fit on the site, and even with a serpentine solution it is difficult to see how Laparelli would have accommodated them. The Manderaggio, that indentation at the southern end of the peninsula, the strange alignment of Fort St Elmo and the position of the northern cavalier (on the site of the present auberge de Castille et Leon) would have made the stock solution unworkable.

Laparelli provided space for a Grand Master's palace as large, he said, as the Palazzo Farnese in Rome, some 6500 square feet in area, with similarly sized plots for the conventual church, the hospital and its ancillary buildings. There were to be eight auberges, or hotels, for the different language groups which formed the Order of St John. The language of England had been suppressed by Henry VIII, but the Knights still lived in hope of seeing it re-established and a space was therefore to be left for its auberge.

There was to be a main square measuring about 260 feet by 195 and one assumes this would front the palace, with smaller squares in front of three public buildings and the eight auberges. Surrounding the whole city there was to be a wide road to serve the fortifications so that troops and guns could be rushed to any quarter of the city that was threatened.

Laparelli tells us he is left with six strips of land running the length of the peninsula, each about 227 feet wide and nearly 1000 yards long. He measured and found that the house of the general of the galleys, a certain Don Pietro, measured 3380 square feet and, assuming this to be an average-sized town house, he estimated that 1125 houses of this size could be built in Valletta on the remaining open ground. He pointed out this was a rough estimate, because no accurate estimate could be made on so hilly a site and the completed job would be a little different from the project. 'More or less', he noted, 'it is enough to know that the site is about three and a half times the size of Il Borgo.'

The executed plan of Valletta differs from Laparelli's project in many respects. Not only was the serpentine pattern of streets abandoned, but the grid-iron was adjusted so that the plots are not uniform in size, although in shape they are rectangular. The main street runs from the city gate to the apex of the nearest bastion in Fort St Elmo and not to its gate; and there are approximately eight longitudinal streets and ten traversing streets. Of the early auberges only that of Aragon has a square in front of it roughly commensurate with Laparelli's suggestion. Nevertheless it does look as though part, if not all, of the present street pattern was laid out by Laparelli before he finally left Malta as we know that building had commenced in the city by that time, and Laparelli has left us an account of the expenses incurred from 21 October 1566 to 22 March 1567 in respect of a house which he had begun to build in Valletta, together with a plan, the design of a room, a window and a well-proportioned doorway.

Throughout Laparelli's stay in Malta the threat of a Turkish invasion hung over the island. Writing on 22 September 1567 Laparelli warned those who thought that the recent estrangement between Constantinople and Venice might divert the Turks' attention away from Malta. 'Big dogs seldom eat each other' he said. 'Money influences people's minds and there are many important merchants on both sides who trade together. They have common interests and will not therefore get very annoyed with each other. In order to demonstrate their strength Venetian and Turk will arm themselves as much as possible and then they will consider the danger less inherent in a way and will reach an agreement. When the Turk has a gun in his hand and is well provisioned, and when he thinks we are not well stocked, it will be a good time for him to attack the island he has always hated. So he will certainly return and will use the suggestion of discord between Turk and Venetian as an excuse to attack Malta.'[14]

Although the Maltese galleys were suitable for use only in summer campaigns when they could be assured of a calm sea, Laparelli must have feared that the Turks could mount a winter campaign against the island. To the Seneschal he wrote – 'Now they fight in winter because what is uncomfortable for one side is also uncomfortable for the enemy. As you know, people have fought well on land and at sea when sometimes one side and sometimes the other has the advantage in winter. People learn how to conquer!'

Near the end of his Codex, Laparelli includes a doleful report by Antonio d'Oria about capturing Valletta. D'Oria claims that the Turk will bring an armada of 30,000 men, capture the island and besiege Valletta. He will easily capture Mdina, the old city in the centre of the island, and Il Borgo and forts St Michael and St Angelo will fall to his assault. Valletta alone remaining will be starved into submission; then all will be lost.

Laparelli's reply is cold and calculated. 'No fortification is an end in itself', he writes. 'When there is a siege it is always necessary to get help from outside, but it is important that the fortifications should resist long enough for the allies to be able to fit out a good relieving army.' Then, flattering the vanity of the Knights, he concluded. 'Everyone knows that Malta is important to Christianity. The island has been called many things including "a thorn in the eye of the Infidel". The Order must always spend a lot of money to defend this island when others have easier tasks. You are

A model of the new city of Valletta showing its land front, with two bastions, two cavaliers behind them and glacis stretching forward into the countryside.

building a new city with all its inconvenience, hoping that if you build it well others will come and settle here. Christendom would have been frightened if it had had to spend as much money as the Order has had to spend on the defence of Malta.'

There were rumours and counter-rumours, Laparelli always pressing for speedy reconstruction, submitting interim reports on progress and estimates for the coming months, and recording the fears and hopes expressed in daily conversation. 'Give me time', he wrote, 'and I will give you life!' His chief assistant, the Maltese architect Gerolamo Cassar, was carefully briefed on the progress of the work and was sent to Italy on a course of architectural instruction. On Cassar's return in 1568 Laparelli applied for winter leave. By the following year the work was well advanced, the street pattern laid down, and already buildings were beginning to rise on the intervening sites. Laparelli was restless – he felt that he had achieved his aims and the work could safely be left in good hands. Consequently he volunteered for service with the Papal fleet wishing to fight against the Turks. He sailed from Malta in 1569, but at Candia, in Crete, he was struck by the plague and soon died. He was 49 years old.

The city of Valletta was built and formed part of the greatest complex of fortifications to come down to us from the Baroque world. Her high bastions and powerful cavaliers are still as Francesco Laparelli left them, defying the passage of time and the onslaught of Hitler's dive-bombers. The city streets still follow the lines he laid out and many of the palaces of the Knights stand as they were erected in the succeeding years.

[1] *Codex of Francesco Laparelli.* c.1565–70, MS. Cortona. Collection Signora Laparelli-Pitti.

[2] This is clearly incorrect. The peninsula is nowhere only 438 yards wide. At its narrowest point, where Laparelli built his front, it is about 880 yards across. A Sicilian canne equals 2·065 metres or approximately six feet seven inches.

[3] Alberti (L. B.) *De re aedificatoria*, Florence 1485, although written in Latin about 1450. An Italian translation was printed by Pietro Lauro in 1546 and Barbaro's popular edition came out in 1550.

[4] For further information on this theme see Wittkower (R.) *Architectural Principles in the Age of Humanism* (London 1952).

[5] It has only now been printed.

[6] *Real Ordenanzas para Nuevos Poblaciones, ecc.,* National Archives, Madrid, M.S. 3017 'Bulas y cedulas para el Govierno de las Indias'. See Nuttall (Zelia) 'Royal Ordinances concerning the laying out of New Towns' in *Hispanic-American Historical Review*, Volume 4 (1921), pages 743–53.

[7] Alberti had quoted from an ancient Roman writer on the most propitious date for commencing to build. 'Frontinus, the architect advised us never to undertake such a work but in a proper season of the year, which is from the beginning of April to the beginning of November.' Book II, chapter xiii.

[8] The Viceroy of Sicily, Ascania della Cornia and the military engineer Fratino arrived on the island and proposed a shorter *enceinte*, probably at the 300 *canne* line. This could account for Laparelli including a design on this line even if he did not himself favour it.

[9] Book V, chapter iv.

[10] Alberti. *Ten Books of Architecture*, English edition translated by James Leoni, Book VI, chapter ii.

[11] *Op. cit.*, Book I, chapter ix.

[12] The italics are mine.

[13] 'Ivor de Wolfe'. *The Italian Townscape* (London 1963), pages 77–88.

[14] On 3 November that year the Grand Master believed that 'the forces of the enemy are twice as strong as they are usually because they have decided to do their utmost against us in order to ruin us this time' and he sent an urgent plea for help to the Duc d'Anjou, brother of the King of France. See Weber (Bernard Clarke), 'an unpublished letter of Jean de la Vallette' in *Melita Historica*, Volume 3, No.1, pages 71–2.

Chapter 4: The Growth of Valletta

By the end of 1566 the rectangular grid plan of the new city of Valletta had been laid out and new buildings began to rise on the sites between the streets. In December of that year the Council carried out a compulsory purchase order on all the land which lay inside Laparelli's fortifications, stretching from the Kingsgate to Fort St Elmo. A Commission consisting of three Knights and three Maltese valued the land and produced a register, so that from 1568 it was possible to purchase plots in the new city for about sixpence a square yard. Town planning control was carried out by the Officio delle Case, a body of long standing and great prestige.[1] This office had to ensure itself that people did not take up sites for speculative purposes and had to prevent undesirable people obtaining sites through nominees. There was a great need to build the city as fast as possible because, once it was occupied, there would be no going back to Il Borgo and Valletta's future, as capital of the island, would be ensured. The Office insisted that where a site was purchased, the building had to be started within six months of the date of purchase and had to be occupied by the end of the year. Town planning regulations were produced which controlled the quality of building and the design of the elevations. These regulations laid down how much money should be spent on each site and insisted that houses should be built up to the street frontages. Those who purchased corner sites were involved in additional expenditure, for the corners had to be ornamented.[2]

The new Grand Master Fra Pietro del Monte, who acceded to the title in 1568, showed particular enthusiasm for the new project. As a gesture of support, on 18 March 1571, with due pomp and circumstance, he moved

the headquarters of the Order from Il Borgo to the new site in Valletta, irrevocably committing the Knights to support of the new citadel, even though its defences were far from finished, were constantly threatened by Turkish invasion and still lacked all the amenities of an established city. The Convent of the Order sailed across the Grand Harbour in richly decor-

The new city of Valletta, from Giacomo Bosio's *Istoria della Sacra Religione di S. Giovanni Gerosolimitano*, Rome 1594 – 1602

ated barges with pennants flying. They made a solemn entry into the new city through the Porta del Monte, now the Kingsgate. The success of the project was assured.

In Rhodes the Knights had lived in a secluded part of the town isolated from the general public by a high wall and reserved exclusively for their habitation. When they moved to Malta and settled in Il Borgo they attempted to reserve an area of the existing town for their exclusive use, but, because they were forced to rent or buy existing property, it was only partially successful. However, in 1562, the Council of the Order did define what they called a collachio area and began to move some of the Maltese out of it. The Vatican was strongly in favour of the Knights maintaining this seclusion and tried to insist upon it by bringing pressure on the Council. When Laparelli produced his original plan he obviously had no intention of dividing the city into two parts, one for the Knights and the other for the Maltese. He allocated sites for the eight residencies or auberges of the various language groups of the Order, each site having a commodious square in front of it. From his recommendations it seems clear that he envisaged distributing the auberges about the city, as a concentration of open squares in one quarter would hardly have made sense. Even in May 1569, two years before the transference of the headquarters from Il Borgo to Valletta, the Council was still working on the idea of dividing the city into two parts, but one feels that this was more a gesture to satisfy Rome than an attempt to impose the rigid seclusion of the life they had known in Rhodes. Rigid seclusion on this site was no longer possible, and the regulations, while allowing the Maltese to live in what was defined as a collachio area, merely ensured that the Knights had the right to obtain property by compulsion in a specified part of Valletta, the terms of the lease to be agreed between them and the lessees.[3]

With the departure and subsequent death of the Italian Francesco Laparelli, the architectural stage was left to Gerolamo Cassar. He had the necessary training and the briefing to undertake the immense task of filling in the space that lay within Laparelli's ring of fortifications with buildings required by the Order in their new capital. It was a golden opportunity for an architect.

Gerolamo Cassar was a Maltese, the first of many to share in the great development of the island as gradually the threat of invasion receded and prosperity came to her people on a scale hitherto unimagined. Cassar was born in Il Borgo in 1520 and was therefore 10 years old when the Knights first arrived. He was active during the great siege, repairing fortifications and inventing war machines, and upon Laparelli's arrival in Malta, Cassar worked with him and provided much of the local knowledge which enabled Laparelli to formulate his plan so speedily.

Some men achieve greatness, others have greatness thrust upon them. When his opportunity came Cassar was about the same age as Bramante had been when he arrived in Rome to lead the Renaissance of the Eternal City. But the situation was very different. From the thirteenth century the Knights of St John had become a brotherhood tuned to the art of war. Its strategy on land and sea had been their sole preoccupation to the exclusion of the graces of life. Although they had made of Rhodes a comfortable abode their aesthetic sensibilities were untuned and, by Western standards, their taste barbaric. What artistic taste filtered through to their leadership had become outmoded when they put it into practice. As fortress builders they were supreme and they lavished all their care and attention to this end. On fortification they sought the best advice available and were prepared to commission and pay for the services of the top-ranking military engineers of Italy and Spain. Francesco Laparelli's involvement with the plan of Valletta was primarily a military assignment. What considerations he took into account on the art of town planning were largely on his own initiative and once the configuration of the fortifications and the distribution of the streets had been articulated, the Knights raised no objection to his request to leave their service and serve elsewhere. But when it came to architecture the Knights were on unsure ground. They preferred to use a local man, probably because it was less costly. They were aware that within the last 100 years at least one artistic revolution had shaken the mainland of Italy and they sought to overcome their inadequacy by despatching their own architectural representative to Italy on a short course of instruction. The Italian admiral of the Order, Pietro del Monte, probably took the initiative. On his elevation to the Grand Mastership he threw himself with enthusiasm into the project of building the new city of Valletta, saw to it that Cassar was admitted as a serving brother in the Italian Langue of the Order, and sent, on 23 April 1569, to study the latest style of architecture in Rome. But in Italy itself the artistic situation was complex. Although most writers on the fine arts had accepted the revolution of the Renaissance which had seemed to sweep away the impurities of the Gothic north and re-establish the tradition of classical design stemming from Imperial Rome, no one had been able to define the psychological situation which had led to the shift in taste we now term Mannerism. Michelangelo was applauded, but remained an enigma. The strange contortions of the architecture of Giulio Romano were envied and even copied by lesser men, but without true comprehension. Mannerism was in the air, but its terms were not defined on paper. When Cassar arrived in Rome, Vignola, the most important and influential architect in the Holy City, was working on the Gesù church. Like many of his compatriots at the time, Vignola was a Mannerist. He had been trained in the classical style, knew all the rules for the correct assembly of the architectural orders and had, in fact, written the standard book on their interpretation. Knowing the rules of composition, he was able to break them as the whim took him, and forge a personal style which was arresting to the eye.

Imagine, however, Gerolamo Cassar's predicament! He was already 49, probably somewhat set in his ideas, and was now catapulted into the midst of a great venture. Whereas Vignola and Michelangelo knew what rules could be broken whilst still achieving an exciting work of architecture, Cassar was scarcely aware of the fact that he was breaking classical rules. This had the result that on his return to Malta, being granted the opportunity of constructing all the important public buildings for the Knights of Valletta, he produced a series of buildings so idiosyncratic in character that they set a pattern which was to cover the whole growth of the new city. Judged as Renaissance works of architecture his buildings are naïve, but because of their powerful expression and their consistency they are most impressive monuments to an Order dedicated to a life of militancy. It may have been his earlier training in fortification architecture which enabled Cassar to impart so forceful an expression to his buildings. And yet what comes from Cassar's drawing board is extraordinarily appropriate, dramatically effective and curiously satisfying. We know the buildings he designed, for they are all listed on a certificate awarded to him by the Grand Master la Cassière: The palace of the Grand Master, the great co-cathedral of St John, the seven auberges or hostels of the various languages of the Order, certain parish churches and convents, the bakeries and the windmills of Valletta.[4] Some were destroyed in the last war, others replaced earlier, but, in spite of this, the extraordinarily powerful imprint of his architecture is responsible for one of the lasting impressions of the city of Valletta. In particular, the rugged blocklike quality of the quoins which bind so many of his buildings stand out with such clarity that one seems to see them at every turn even though there can be no more than a dozen in the city. These are the hallmark of his architecture – a curious trait and one wonders where he picked it up. Probably not during his visit to Italy as these quoins are not a peculiarity of Rome. They may have been implanted in his mind at an early date and rested there like a fixation. Ten years earlier Bartolomeo Genga had visited Malta and had interested the Knights in a project for building a new city on Mount Sceberras, where Valletta now stands. He is reported to

The palace of the Grand Masters in Valletta.

have prepared designs for some churches and a magisterial palace which may have influenced Cassar. Genga was a master in the use of heavy rustication. We also know that Laparelli prepared a drawing of a house in 1566 with a rusticated corner, but Gerolamo Cassar's handling of thc quoins is very personal. His quoins vary from building to building but always retain the bold, deep-cut form, the long, harshly projected slab and the exaggerated proportions which make them so much of an eye-catcher.

The Magisterial palace in Kingsway is usually considered Cassar's least successful building, possibly because it was a conversion from a smaller house. Originally it was intended that the palace should be on the Castille heights, but in order to get things moving the Grand Master purchased a house from his nephew in the centre of the city and commissioned Cassar to enlarge it and make it more magnificent. Remnants of the original house can still be seen on the north-west corner of the main façade. The quoins there are much smaller than those Cassar uses elsewhere and the windows are bunched closer together. Cassar's extension was on a more generous scale and for many years the roofline of the original house was lower than that on the rest of the building. There appears to be no clear rhythm to the spacing of the windows and Cassar originally provided only one gateway, placed asymmetrically on the façade. The Baroque embellishments to the gateways, and the long balconies which project on their elaborately carved stone consoles were added in the eighteenth century, relieving what must have been a comparatively plain façade. The palace is designed around a central courtyard, later sub-divided into two by the introduction of a long corridor, and the main accommodation is on the first floor in the Italian fashion. There are richly apparelled rooms and sumptuous decorations. Most of the ceilings are constructed in timber, an unusual feature in Malta, as all the beams had to be imported from Sicily, and the joists are corbelled from the walls in a manner similar to that used by the Knights in Rhodes. The Hall of St Michael and St George is the most magnificent room in the building. It has always created a powerful impression on visitors and Tiepolo chose to depict it in a fresco which is now in the museum at Udine.[5] Brydone, visiting Valletta in the eighteenth century, noted that the 'Palace is a very noble though a plain structure, and the Grand Master (who studies conveniency more than magnificence) is more comfortably and commodiously lodged than any prince in Europe, the King of Sardinia perhaps only excepted. The great stair is by much the easiest and best I ever saw.'[6] The walls of the hall are hung in red damask and lined with large mirrors and the frieze, painted by Matteo Perez d'Aleccio, a pupil of Michelangelo, depicts with magnificent gusto the Great Siege of Malta.

The auberges of the Knights were distributed around the city, each housing members drawn from a particular language group and each placed near to its respective curtain of fortification to be defended by its Knights. The auberges provided communal living like the Oxford and Cambridge colleges, the Knights being obliged to dine in hall at least four times a week.

The auberge d'Aragon, begun in 1571, was probably the first to be built. It is a plain structure with a central courtyard, its elevations the result of a compromise on Cassar's part where he is patently trying to achieve irregularity of spacing of the windows inside the rooms and a regular rhythm on the façade. A year earlier Palladio had published his *Quattro libri dell' architettura* which contained his researches into this very problem. In Palladio's villas around Vicenza in northern Italy he was able to integrate the internal and external proportions of his buildings in a way that no one had done before. One can see Cassar probing at the problem without complete success throughout his architectural development.

The auberge d'Italie was begun in 1574, together with the adjoining church of St Catherine of the Langue of Italy, whose exterior has now been refurbished. The auberge has a square courtyard in the Italian style and originally consisted of one main floor with a semi-basement, its roof line coming where the string course between ground floor and first floor now lies. It must have been a typical Cassar design, long and low, framed with immensely powerfully carved quoins at each corner. The vigorously rusticated doorway is probably also by Cassar, but the elaborate carved cartouche of the arms of the Grand Master Carafa, with its paraphernalia of flags and pennants, trumpets and guns, all assembled within the damask hangings of a proscenium arch, date from the last years of the seventeenth century. This rich Baroque carving comes easily from the Maltese stone and its addition to numerous buildings in the city creates an ever-changing chiaroscuro, which enlivens the long straight streets of Laparelli's grid plan. The auberge de Provence, now the museum and once the Union Club of the British armed forces, is much the most mature of Cassar's designs, so much so that some doubt its authenticity, suggesting that the front has been refaced

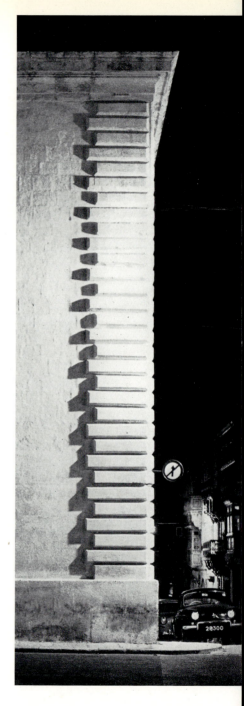

Left: Cassar's quoins on the auberge d'Aragon.

Right: The escutcheons of the Grand Master Vilhena above the doorway of the auberge of the Italian Knights at Valletta.

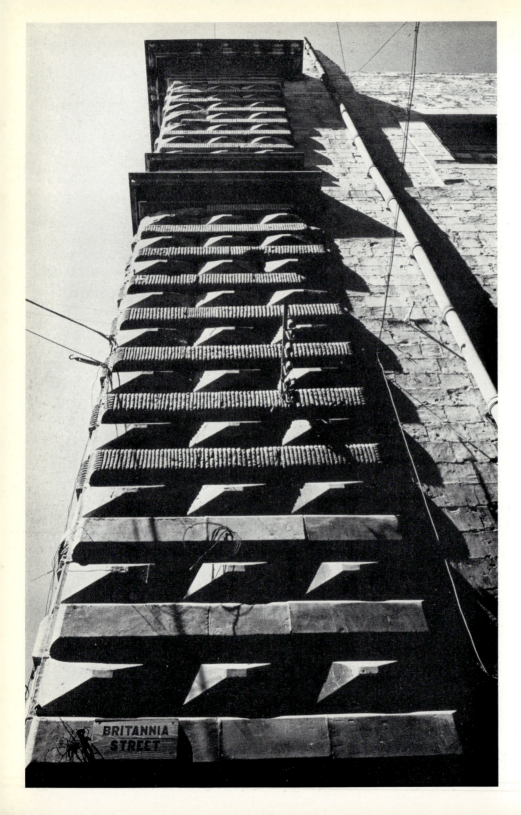

Left: Powerful quoins support the corner of the auberge d'Italie.

Right: Gerolamo Cassar's quoins on the auberge de Provence in Valletta.

Left: The elevation of the destroyed auberge de France in Valletta.

Right: Cassar's church of St Augustine at Rabat, built in 1571.

in the seventeenth century. It has a columnal design with a strange up and down rhythm as the eye is forced to rise over each pedestal supporting coupled pilasters and then drop on the adjoining window frame. It is symmetrical and has a regular rhythm, the symmetricality being emphasized by a centrepiece, an ingeniously paraphrased Roman triumphal arch, a little temple piece which seems squeezed between two segmental pediments supported on columns more widely spaced than the adjoining pilasters. Cassar's bulky quoins are at their mightiest, with the result that the rest of the façade seems more playful than anything he has used before, but the game is kept strictly within bounds by the demarcation of the weighty quoins. This auberge has a richly painted, barrel-vaulted entrance leading to a staircase which rises to a gallery whose balustrade seems hung from wall to wall at cornice level.

As he progressed Cassar developed a knack, almost an intuition, for handling voids and solids. It is sad that the auberge de France was destroyed in the last war for we have lost so much of Cassar in this destruction. He designed for it an asymmetrical façade handled with gusto and bravado. This conscious asymmetrical planning belongs at the earliest to the Romantic Revival and more fully to our own times, and yet we cannot doubt the authenticity of this design nor, on the evidence, can we doubt that Cassar's design was fully premeditated. It is therefore quite outside its period – a remarkable precursor.

St John's, Valletta, the co-cathedral and the mother church of the Knights of Malta, is Cassar's most impressive building. But first he did a trial run at Rabat where he was set a test piece by the Augustinians before being allowed to embark on his chef d'œuvre. This test, the church of St Augustine, was commenced in 1571. The façade is a screen, built to hide the paraphernalia of the construction which lies behind, and, at the same time,

Left: The interior of St Augustine's
church showing later decoration.

Right: The conventual church of St John
in Valletta.

to weld into an architectural unity the disproportionate dimensions of nave
and side chapels, a problem already well chewed over by the architects of
Renaissance Rome. On to the screen Cassar projects a series of Mannerist
devices like the breaking up of the string course over the central door.[7]
There is much which suggests some half-remembered impression of Vignola's Gesù in Rome. The nave and choir of St Augustine's church have
four bays roofed with a slightly arched barrel vault. A thickened rib in this
vault is the only indication of the cessation of the nave and the commence-
ment of the chancel – a strange device Cassar later uses on St John's,
Valletta. The interior is weighty and robust, the capitals of the bulky doric
pilasters form, without the imposition of an entablature, the springing for
the arched roof. Cavernous side chapels, their cross vaults strongly coffered,
reach out from the tubby half-columns which flank the nave pilasters. Despite all its ungainly proportions, the interior of St Augustine's has an impressive directness and a confident boldness which must have endeared it
to his patrons and gained for Cassar the confidence and trust of the Order
embarking upon the construction of its most important monument.

St John's, Valletta, is one of the strangest and yet one of the most impressive churches in Christendom. Its exterior has all the qualities of the
citadel it represents – its interior is an uncompromising vaulted cavern overlaid with an extraordinary sumptuousness of carved stone and paint. The
main front, packed with Mannerist details, is unusual by Italian standards,
for it has two western towers which flank a central screen covering the nave
and aisles. Several Italian architects have proposed this solution and Serlio
in Book V of his treatise on architecture[8] illustrates a rather similar solution.

At the time of Cassar's visit to Italy, the two leading Italian architects, Palladio and Vignola, were obsessed with this very problem, the incorporation of two towers in a façade – Palladio in the chapel at Maser and Vignola in his unexecuted designs for the Gesù and Sant' Anna dei Palafrenieri in Rome. It is possible that Cassar envisaged the addition of the two wings which continue the street frontage for the width of the block and contribute so much to the fort-like quality of the co-cathedral. These additions were made shortly after his death. There was also some evidence to suggest that Cassar originally intended adding a dome and possibly transepts at the eastern end of the present church, although this would have entailed closing one of the crossing streets of Valletta and extending the church into the next block. Fortunately this step was not taken and the direct, powerful, lineal quality of the interior remains undamaged by the introduction of cross axes. For two centuries after Cassar's death the Knights continued to embellish their great church. The marble floor pattern was slowly built up with the elaborate memorial tablets to commemorate their dead. The vault was painted in the five years beginning in 1662 by the Italian painter Mattia Preti working in oil straight on to the primed stone-work of the ceiling with scenes of power and verve, and the various languages of the Order, each of which was allocated one side chapel, vied with each other to provide rich and elaborate decoration, costly paintings and consummate works of sculpture.[9] The great, uninterrupted drive of the nave leads the eye to the radiating marble group of the 'Baptism of Christ' set in the recessed apse, executed by Giuseppe Mazzuoli, which rises in splendid fiery form above Lorenzo Gafà's cathedra. Gafà was one of the most accomplished Maltese architects of the seventeenth century and his best work can be seen in the parish churches and the cathedrals of Mdina and Gozo.

Gerolamo Cassar died in 1586 and was buried in the vaults of the church he designed for the Augustinians at Rabat. An engraving of him exists, but one wonders how truthfully it portrays his character. It shows a dark-haired man with hair brushed forward on to the forehead, a thin face with high cheek bones and restless eyes. A heavy pouchy moustache, perhaps to give him confidence – a front to the uncertainties which must have plagued his creativity. He is wearing a ruff with some apparent discomfort. That he was a remarkable man no one can doubt for, in a matter of a few years, he forged his own peculiar style and pressed it home in the creation of a large number of impressive buildings which were to colour the subsequent development of Maltese architecture.

In comparison, contemporary buildings in Valletta were conservative in the extreme, continuing to use the heavy rolling mouldings which the Knights had used on their buildings in Il Borgo. There are a number of houses in Valletta which still cling to this outmoded form of expression and the great hospital of the Order, one of the two foremost of its time in the provision of medical services, is stylistically retrograde.

By 1582 few vacant sites remained in the new city of Valletta and ten years later the population had risen to nearly 4000. An English visitor commented in his diary in the year 1610 that 'the city is now almost absolutely finished'.[10]

Valletta was becoming so successful that the old cities on the other side of the Grand Harbour were reduced nearly to slums and the archives of the Order described how 'the houses of the soldiers of the garrison to Fort St Angelo are now, as everybody knows, in such a bad state that they are not fit for habitation without being exposed to the inclemency of the weather and the rigours of the season. Not only that, but also being in continuous and imminent danger of losing your lives and to be buried under the threatening and irreparable ruins of the same. . . . from the basements to their roofs there is nothing good, sound or resisting, whether it is the walls, for the greater part already fallen to the ground and the remaining parts falling and loose, or the roofs which are altogether so cracked that not only do they no longer offer shelter from the rain, but, drinking in the water and being thoroughly soaked, they continually drip after the rain for several days, which is more harmful and annoying than the rain itself.'[11]

The old capital of Mdina was being slowly drained of its population. Few but the ancient Maltese families remained, sulking in their isolation and building up grievances against those Knights who had occupied their land.

As Valletta grew, her demand for water increased. In 1610 the Grand Master, Alof de Wignacourt, commissioned an aqueduct to be built to carry water from the foothills to the city nine and a half miles away. At the Floriana staging post the water line is marked by a fine buttressed tower carrying upon it the carved arms of the Grand Master. Originally two Italian engineers had been commissioned to carry out the work, but the Grand Master, dissatisfied with their progress, sacked them and appointed the Maltese architect Giovanni Attard to do the job.

Right: Cassar's façade of St John's church.

Overleaf, page 94:
Monument to the Grand Master Nicolas Cotoner in St John's.

Overleaf, page 95:
The nave and chancel of St John's.

Left: The de la Salle palace in Valletta, built about 1600, still retains 'fat' mouldings around the windows.

Right: A staging post and fountain on the line of the Wignacourt aqueduct at Floriana.

The city rose rapidly, its buildings at that time mainly of two stories topped with flat roofs, their cubic quality merging with the long, horizontal lines of the fortifications, broken only by the few church towers of such buildings as St John's and the Carmelite convent.

In the seventeenth and eighteenth centuries Valletta added embellishments to her dress and became a Baroque city. Gradually the threat of a major invasion receded, the Order prospered, the population expanded and the Knights turned to more leisurely pursuits. Valletta slowly changed from a city of soldiers to a city of gentlemen. The power of the Turkish fleet waned after its defeat at the battle of Lepanto in 1571, but sporadic raids continued to be made on Malta in the seventeenth century. There was the landing of 1614, for instance, which caused havoc and desolation in the countryside. An armada consisting of 200 large warships and many ancillary vessels was fitted out in Constantinople in preparation for a major assault on Malta in 1639, but the expedition was abandoned on the death of the sultan. The story of the invasion preparations comes from a contemporary Turkish chronicler and, although his description of the size of the invasion fleet was probably exaggerated, doubtless a serious invasion was contemplated.[12]

Palaces built in Valletta in the first half of the seventeenth century are comparatively plain, their windows set in large plain areas of wall and decorated with rolls of traditional Maltese mouldings. The de la Salle palace is a typical example. Built on a sloping site, it is heavily buttressed at the corners with rusticated quoins which give way to a plain pilaster above the projecting lace-like balconies. The other windows seem to be disposed quite arbitrarily along the length of the façade. The first-floor windows have their hood mouldings detached from the window architraves and the main door is set at the upper end of the building opening on to an easy staircase which leads to the main living rooms on the first floor. The entrance has a circular window above it, a feature found on many of these early Valletta palaces, and the hood moulding of the door has consequently been pushed well above this circular window, so that it serves no real purpose. The façade is whimsical, but not without a certain charm. It is a reminder of the character which Valletta must have displayed throughout the first half of the seventeenth century.

Then came the change with the importation of Bernini's Baroque style from Rome. The church of St James is an admirable example of this. It has

a fine moulded façade of two stories, richly conceived but with the embellishments controlled and the carving never allowed to run to seed. Also, like Roman Baroque work, this is a characteristic of Maltese sculpture, surprising when one considers the ease with which the local limestone can be cut and shaped. Unlike many examples in Spain and Sicily, Maltese sculpture rarely over-ripens, dripping its juices uncontrollably across the façades of these buildings. The doors and window frames of St James's church are elegantly carved and the crowning cartouche over the central window is particularly magnificent, with outstretched wings supporting the framed coat of arms. The church was built in 1710 by Giovanni Barbara, one of the most competent Maltese Baroque architects, and, replacing an earlier structure, it was used as the conventional church of the Langue of Castille.

Magnificent carving of trophies, banners, arms, and armour
surround the swaggering bust of the Portuguese Grand Master
Emanuel Pinto on the façade of the auberge shown opposite.

Domenico Cachia's brilliant auberge for
the Knights of Castille and Leon in
Valletta.

The Hotel de Vedelin, though earlier, is more florid and shows a strong Sicilian influence. It faces on to the palace square and is in sharp contrast to the austere character of the palace and the main guard. Baroque buildings sprang up everywhere in the city. One of the most representative examples, the archbishop's palace, with its rich columnal doorway and its hard edge mouldings, is seen to best effect in the street lighting of the night when the shadows are thrown out and up across the façade.

The traditional cubic quality of the Maltese houses is retained, in many cases, and the only significant departure from earlier practice is the addition of elaborate sculpture around the windows and the use of richly carved stone corbels to support a lace-like balcony. Such a contrast can be seen on the offices of the British Council, an eighteenth-century building which adjoins a much earlier house whose windows are still decorated with the traditional Maltese 'fat' moulding.

Merchants street is particularly rich in buildings of this period. The Municipal palace was built about 1720, a two-storey structure with shops on the ground floor, a powerfully shaped doric portal, richly carved headpieces to the first floor windows and an elaborate centrepiece depicting a draped cloak. The Castellania, which was begun by the Maltese architect Francesco Zerafa in 1748 and completed by Giuseppe Bonici in 1760, housed the civil and criminal courts. The corners of the building are strongly buttressed with carved pilasters, the main cornice is bold and the centre of the façade is built up to contain the carved figures of 'Justice' and 'Truth' fashioned by the Sicilian sculptor Maestro Gian.

The new auberge of the Langue of Castille et Leon is the high-water mark of Maltese Baroque. It replaced Gerolamo Cassar's earlier auberge on the Castille heights, the most commanding position for any building in the city. It was designed by a brilliant Maltese architect, Domenico Cachia, who was also responsible for the design of the parish church of St Helen at Birkirkara. He began the auberge when he was 44 and lived to the ripe old age of 90. Little is known of his life but he must have visited Sicily and southern Italy for the inspiration of the auberge de Castille. His model is clearly the Prefettura at Lecce, in the heel of Italy, but Cachia's work surpasses this. The façade is rich, yet not over-ornate, and has pleasing proportions. The rhythm of pilaster, recessed panel, and centrepiece projection is enlivening, and the recessed rustication of the ground floor gives the build-

Above: The Municipal palace.

Right: The customs house in Valletta, designed by Giuseppe Bonici in 1774.

ing a solidity which is needed because of the large wall surface above the main floor windows. There is a rich central focus created by the elaborate build-up of the carved staircase to a central door, the splaying out of the columns of the portal and the magnificent carving of trophies, banners, arms, and armour which surround the swaggering bust of the Portuguese Grand Master Emanuel Pinto. Pinto was the first Grand Master to assume regal

Left and right: Streets in Valletta. 'We walked up streets which were long flights of stairs, admired balconies and the innumerable bits of picturesque architecture and varied outline that everywhere met the eye and seemed so tasteful when compared with the pasteboard rows of prosaic streets, which are built by contract and squeezed into stupid shape by our city authorities.' From the letter of a Scottish traveller in 1864.

magnificence and adopt in his coat of arms the closed crown of the monarchy. Everything about his office proclaimed this pomp and extravagant expression, and most particularly does this Castillian building reflect his attitude. The crescent moon, his armorial symbol, is liberally disposed about the building and his coat of arms forms the climax of the central window, overlaid on a field of cannon and banners. Pinto's long reign, from 1741 to 1773, illustrates the change of taste which took place in Valletta by means of its many building projects. The Knights switched from their traditional role of soldier and sailor, now ostentatiously patronizing the arts to express the glory of the Order. The city was embellished with rich buildings, carved fountains and elaborate statuary.[13]

In 1731 the Manoel theatre was begun. It is a delightful design, still in use and one of the oldest theatres in Europe. Its auditorium, modelled on the theatre at Palermo, has three floors of boxes which run in a continuous sweep from the proscenium arch.

But always present, overshadowing the scene, are the fortifications of Valletta. Accretioned, hacked out, cut into, converted or insulted by the rude army huts of corrugated iron, they still rise above this meanness, sublimely magnificent. Though perhaps some of the quality has departed. An English visitor in 1864 described the scene. 'We wandered along battery upon battery, passed innumerable rows of big guns which had pyramids of shot beside them, and which looked down white precipices, as if watching the deep harbour which washed their base, and sorrowing that they had nothing to do. We saw forts – forts everywhere, forts on this side, forts on the other side, forts above us and forts below us.'[14]

1 Mifsud (A.) *Knights Hospitallers of the Venerable Tongue of England in Malta* (Malta 1916).

2 Blouet (B. W.) 'Town Planning in Malta 1530–1798' in *The Town Planning Review*, Volume 35 (October 1964).

3 A.O.M. Liber Conciliorum, Volume 92, fo. 137.

4 A.O.M. Liber Bullarum, Volume 1439, fo.270.

5 For a good description of the palace see Sammut (Edward). *The Palace of the Grand Masters* (Malta 1952).

6 Brydone (P.) *A Tour through Sicily and Malta in a series of letters to William Beckford, Esq. of Somerly in Suffolk* (London 1773), page 318.

7 Some of the details of the façade look as though they were done by another architect. For further evidence see Quentin Hughes, *The Building of Malta*, pages 61–2.

8 *Quinto libro dell'architettura di Sebastiano Serlio* (Venice 1566).

9 Scicluna (Sir Hannibal) *The Church of St John in Valletta* (Rome 1955)

10 Sandys (George) *A Relation of a journey begun Anno. Dom. 1610 Four Books containing a description of the Turkish Empire, of Egypt, of the Holy Land, of the remoter parts of Italy, etc.* (London 1615), page 232.

11 A.O.M. Volume 1016 (29 October 1692).

12 Pullicino (J. Cassar). 'A Turkish Expedition against Malta in 1639' in *Scientia*, Volume 17, No.3 (1951), pages 109–15.

13 For an interesting description of the growth of Valletta see Tonna (Joseph A.) 'Valletta – an amalgam of Four Centuries' in *Sunday Times of Malta* (27 March, 3 April, 10 April 1966).

14 Pullicino (J. Cassar). 'Valletta by Moonlight – a description made by Norman Macleod during a visit to Malta in 1864' from *Sunday Times of Malta* (16 December 1956).

Chapter 5: The Outer Defences

This Maltese cannon, made in 1680, has a length of 8 feet and a bore of $5\frac{1}{2}$ inches.

Meanwhile, the work of aggrandisement went ahead with the slow but sure construction of ring upon ring of defences for the islands of Malta and Gozo. The enlargement of the enceinte was dictated by two things. First, by the sheer thirst for dilation that characterizes the Baroque and provided in its town planning and fortification projects a forum for the pomp and display of the regal world of the West. And second, through a definite and practical need to overcome the problem of the long-range gun. The sixteenth and seventeenth centuries saw a rapid increase in the effectiveness of gunfire. A twelve-pounder gun was lethal at a point blank range of about 300 yards and had an effective range of 1400 yards when the gun was elevated to an angle of four degrees. Similarly an eighteen-pounder could hit at 360 yards point blank, and at 1600 yards when elevated. Mortars, too, came into regular use as they could pinpoint a target. Royals and Clehorns could fire up to 600 yards. Turkish artillery was particularly effective, largely due to the number of heavy calibre guns they deployed. On the eastern front, weapons of 80 to 120-pound calibre were quite common, but in an attack on Malta the carrying capacity of the fleet and the manoeuvrability of the weapons were a consideration to be borne in mind by the Turks. The Knights could take no chances and it became clear that, with the longer range of the guns, the early defences of Valletta and the Three Cities on the other side of the Grand Harbour, Il Borgo, rechristened Vittoriosa, Isola, now Senglea, and Bormla, now Cospicua, could be outflanked by guns on higher positions.

In order to appreciate the problems of the Knights of Malta it is neces-

A 5-inch bronze cannon built for the Grand Master Emanuel Pinto in 1756. Stands outside the auberge de Castille et Leon in Valletta.

sary to understand something of the art of attack and defence and the way in which Baroque engineers tried to solve these problems. A war is fought out in terms of strategy and tactics and it is important to understand the distinction between these two terms. Strategy is the large-scale plan – the overall method proposed for the winning of the war. It is a concept that needs time for its realization and all permanent lines of fortification should be the result of this strategic plan. It was the task of a war council, in this case headed by the Grand Master, to assess the main risks to which Malta and Gozo were likely to be subjected by the Turks and to act accordingly. Strategy is upset by tactics which exploit the situation not anticipated, and carry this exploitation to a successful conclusion. Tactics are the art of manoeuvring the forces once the battle has commenced – the method of outwitting an opponent and of tackling a difficult situation. The commander might use tactics in playing against the rules of the game – for there are rules to the art of war. As far as fortification is concerned, it is often the unexpected exploitation of a situation, the odds of which have not been correctly weighed up by the besieged, that is a danger into which many strategists fall. It is to this danger that nearly all permanent lines of fortification from Troy to the Siegfried Line eventually succumb. Successful lines of fortification like the Maginot Line are those which are never put to the test. Into this category fall the fortifications of Valletta and the Three Cities, with their numerous curtains and bastions built mile upon mile. They were never tested. They faced outwards but never received the brunt of the attack against which they were designed. Although the Turk often returned to skirmish he never came back in a force sufficiently powerful to threaten the Knights' suzerainty of the islands and their power collapsed only when their defences were outflanked and attacked insidiously by a fifth column organized with subtle care by the French Knights and augmented by the forces of Napoleon. It might, therefore, be argued that all the sweat and toil to cut the stones and heap the ramparts, all the diplomacy to borrow and collect the money and the colossal expenditure with its consequent drain on the Maltese exchequer, were wasted and of no avail. But this is not true. The sheer fact that the fortress was not again assaulted and was garrisoned for over two centuries with a comparatively meagre defending force, is witness to the effectiveness of the art of the military engineer. His work was a deterrent.

To counteract the effect of the increased range of the guns it was necessary to push the defences farther out and so increase the area of fortified ground between the cities and the front lines which might be occupied by the Turks. At first sight it would appear to create a problem in that the bigger the field covered by permanent fortifications, the larger the garrison needed to defend it. But this is not so! One must realize that the Turkish manpower was also restricted by the number of soldiers it was feasible to bring on the ships and that the Turks would have to circle the lines of the Maltese fortifications. It would, therefore, be impossible for them to attack everywhere and they would have to concentrate on one or two points. Bearing in mind the fact that distances inside the fortifications were always less than those outside, it would always be quicker for the Knights to switch their defence from one point to another than for the Turks to switch their attack. It meant, of course, that the Knights had to be provided with excellent lines of communication and suitable places for assembling troops to meet a sudden shift in the direction of the attack.

A visitor is always impressed by the immensity of the Valletta fortifications. Coleridge called them 'bulky mountain breasted heights', but extreme height is not always a great advantage. The walls are themselves exposed and vulnerable to bombardment, and guns placed on their ramparts can only carry out what is called plunging fire, where the cannon balls fall on the heads of the attackers. This is not as effective as sweeping fire where the ball rebounds and ricochets many hundreds of times, like a flat stone skimming along the surface of the water. With plunging fire the ball is often embedded in the ground or bounces too high and wastes its energy. Ricochet was first effectively used at Philipsburg in 1688, but did not become common practice until the eighteenth century.

The art of defence consisted in the ability to economize with soldiers so that a garrison could resist a much more powerful attacking force. This was achieved in three ways. First, by providing cover so that the defenders could not be observed and shot at. Second, by making the position as inaccessible as possible, obstructed and difficult to approach. And third, by giving the defence the advantage of height, so that its soldiers are able to observe the enemy without themselves being observed. The first essential then was cover, and for this a parapet had to be constructed high enough to cover the tallest man and thick enough to stop the heaviest shot likely to be thrown at

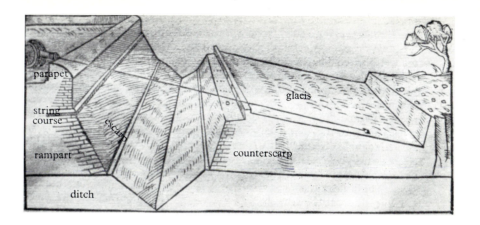

it. Parapets were usually constructed about eight feet high to provide cover against shot pitching over the crest. They varied in thickness. Three feet was sufficient to stop musketry, but about eighteen feet of earth or masonry was needed to withstand the pounding from an eighteen-pounder gun. Behind the parapet lay the rampart, along which the soldiers passed, and the banquette, a step upon which they raised themselves to fire over the crest of the parapet. In front of the parapet a ditch was dug to make it less accessible. The outer face of the parapet is called the escarp and the outer face of the ditch the counterscarp. Ditches could either be filled with water or left dry, and many of the early treatises on the art of fortification discuss at length the merits of these two systems. However, as the design of fortifications was pushed farther and farther forward, and the perimeter began to be defended with small outworks which could take the brunt of the initial attack, the dry ditch became more popular. One can understand this, for troops occupying the outworks would not like to face the prospect of swimming across the ditches when they were withdrawn to the main fortifications. In addition, large dry ditches provided places for the Knights to assemble both reconnaissance parties and striking forces, their activities concealed from the Turks. A defence should never be static and the most effective defence is that which is augmented by sudden offensive strikes which take the enemy off balance. Beyond the ditches the Knights constructed glacis. These were made by raising the level of the ground immediately in front of the ditch so that it could be seen by soldiers on the ram-

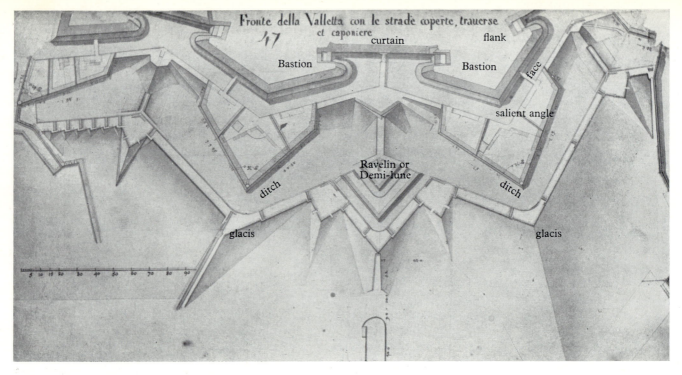

Bastion

curtain

flank

Bastion

face

salient angle

Ravelin or
Demi-lune

ditch

ditch

glacis

glacis

Part of the land front of Valletta.

parts without their having to lean over the crest of the parapet and expose themselves to Turkish fire.

This then is the basis of a defensive line, but numerous refinements had to be incorporated in its shaping, in the lines it followed on the ground and in its detailed arrangement. Traversing platforms, for instance, had to be provided so that the guns could be swung round to fire in different directions. Barbettes had to be built behind the guns so that they could not be raked from the flanks by Turkish fire. Embrasures had to be cut in the parapet. These consisted of a neck through which the gun fired and splayed cheeks so that it could be swung round to fire in an arc. Embrasures had their disadvantages, for although they protected the guns they restricted their use and they also tended to act as a funnel for enemy shot. These cuts also tended to weaken the parapet so that it might be damaged either by enemy fire or from the concussion of the defending guns. And, of course, embrasures pinpointed the position of the defending guns.

The pattern in which the fortifications were laid out on the ground was called the trace and was evolved as the result of an advanced knowledge of geometry. One suspects that some designers were carried away by the sheer beauty of its delineation, but one must realize that it was more than an exercise in geometry. A wrong decision and a faulty line meant at the very least the death of a precious soldier and, more probably, a weak link in the chain of defence through which, once snapped, the enemy would pour its forces and overcome the defence. The history of war is the history of strategic miscalculations, of towns put to the sword, of women and children butchered. One cannot afford mistakes, and the Knights were at great pains to employ the best brains to solve their problems. All the major treatises on fortification were studied with great care and many of the most notable military engineers visited Malta in order to give their advice to the Knights.

In the sixteenth century Italian military engineers held the field, their art learnt from the treatises of Alberti and Francesco di Giorgio. They were pre-eminent and their services sought by the princes of Europe. Although some of their erudition was the result of book learning, most of their expertise was acquired the hard way, practice on the field of battle often under hazardous conditions. The Italian battlefront; war in Central Europe as the forces of the Holy Roman Empire faced the onslaught of the Turks; battles in North Africa with Charles's Spanish troops; and the containment of the Low Countries, as the Duke of Alva ruthlessly held in a grip of iron the Spanish Netherlands; all provided ample opportunity for architects and engineers. Most of the fighting was bloody and without quarter given, the risks high and the need paramount to provide adequate defence. Statements by men like the Duke of Alva help us to realize the full implications of the threat to life and the need to show no stint in the provision of defensive works around the towns of Europe. In 1573, when work on the Valletta fortification was going ahead with great rapidity, Alva remarked: 'If I take Alkmaar I am resolved not to leave a single creature alive; the knife shall be put to every throat.' Manuals flowed from the pens of the Italian theorists, men like Machiavelli, Nicola Tarteglia, Francesco de Marchi, Jacopo Castriotto and Gerolomo Maggi, and demonstrate the demand. It was said that Francesco de Marchi's *Dell' architettura militare libri tre*, which was published in 1546, became very rare because, according to the Italians, foreign engineers destroyed copies of this book to conceal their own plagiarism. Gerolomo Maggi is a typical military engineer of the period. He was born in Anghiari, in the centre of Italy, and in 1571 was engaged on the defence of Famagusta in Cyprus, where the Turks under Suleiman II had switched their attack after the unsuccessful siege of Malta. Commanded by Marc Antonio Bragadino, the garrison consisted of some 7000 men, half Italian, half Greek. The attack showed all the ferocity to be expected from the Turks, and only when the magazines were empty and the ramparts a continuous mass of ruins did the commander agree to surrender the remnant of his force. The Turkish general, the Mustapha Pasha who had been in Malta and was still stinging from the indignity of his reversal there, granted Bragadino honourable terms of surrender, but no sooner had the garrison laid down its arms than the Turks violated these terms with great ferocity. Bragadino was mutilated and put to death, Maggi was taken a prisoner and sold as a slave in Constantinople. There he attempted to escape but was recaptured and strangled in his prison in May 1572. The events of Maggi's life were not exceptional. Many military engineers were killed on the battlefield in the prime of life, or died in some distant prison.

In the seventeenth century French engineers were pre-eminent, the wars of Louis XIV providing adequate opportunity for employment. Men like Errard of Bar-le-duc, de Ville, Fabré, the Count de Pagan, who visited Malta, and, most notable of all, Sébastien le Prestre de Vauban who, in recognition of his services, was raised to the rank of Marshal of France in 1703.

But to return to Malta. By the 1570s the defences of Valletta were nearing completion. A ring of high walls stood around the city, supported to landward by the four star-shaped bastions, their points thrust forward into the countryside beyond. Between the bastions lay three curtain walls, the middle one pierced by the main gate of the city, the Porto St Giorgio, later called Kingsgate. Above the bastions stood cavaliers, four projected and two completed – raised polygonal forts providing full command of the ground which would otherwise have been imperfectly seen from the ramparts, and providing additional range for the defending guns of the city of Valletta. Francesco Laparelli had done his work well and for nearly seventy years no further fortifications were carried out in Malta.

In 1632 Pietro Paolo Floriani was invited to Malta to discuss the possibility of strengthening the land front of Valletta by increasing its depth towards the Marsa. His name was well known on the island. His father

Pompeii Floriani had been a notable writer on the art of fortification, and had published a book in 1576 criticizing Laparelli's defences of Valletta.[1] The father died when young Floriani was 15, but the environment had already had its effect and young Floriani drew profit from his father's cognizance, experience won in fighting at Lepanto, and practical proficiency gained at numerous fortresses. Young Floriani, within the aura created by the fame and success of his father, threw himself into a study of battle tactics and in particular military architecture. He was tutored by men who had

Harbour and fortifications of Valletta, taken from the survey of the French engineers.

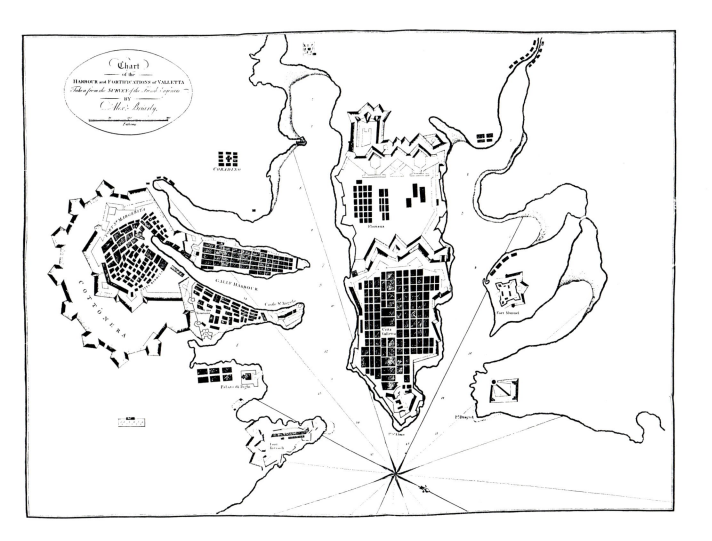

built reputations for themselves in the wars in Flanders, Hungary, and the Levant. Soon he was involved in his own practice, building fortifications in Italy. He entered the service of the king of Spain and carried out a secret mission to assess the feasibility of capturing the Turkish cities of Algiers and Tunis. In 1620 he was with the Imperial Army at the siege of Rosenburg and in the following year took part in the assault on Neuhäusel. Leading 200 men he personally stormed the towns of Valcodero, la Cola, and San Giorgio, and built so great a name for bravery that sonnets were written in his praise. By 1627 he was Castellan of Fort St Angelo in Italy and Governor of the armies of Umbria. At this time he began to compile his experience into his great tome on fortification.[2] With this reputation it is little wonder that his work should be heeded by the Knights. In Malta he criticized the Laparelli defences on five scores. The land defence was not spacious enough to keep an enemy at a distance. In front of the main gate there was insufficient area screened from the view of the enemy; nor was the ditch wide enough to allow an adequate counter-attacking party to be assembled. The flanks of the front were weak. The ditch was too deep and too narrow, and the parapets above too wide to allow the guns to fire down into the ditch. And finally there was lack of provision for ammunition in the bastions so that the guns could not be rapidly reloaded.[3] In 1635 Floriani visited Malta and recommended the construction of an elaborate trace of fortifications stretching across the neck of the peninsula at approximately 800 canne from Fort St Elmo.

It will be remembered that this was the third position for the front recommended by Laparelli which had been ruled out because it enclosed too large an area for the city of Valletta. But Floriani's proposals had a different objective and resulted from the increased effectiveness of gunfire developed in the seventeenth century. They were to blunt the spearhead of the Turkish attack and to withhold, or delay, an assault on Laparelli's land front. Floriani's fortifications were to be placed on the edge of the plateau looking out over the low ground at the Marsa. In essence they consisted of three lines of defence. The innermost line was made up of three main pointed, or angular, constructions called bastions. Between each lay a curtain wall pierced by a gate. The northern gate called The gate of Our Lady has now been destroyed. The southern gate, the Porte des Bombes, was later extended when the arch was doubled and the adjoining curtain walls cut away to

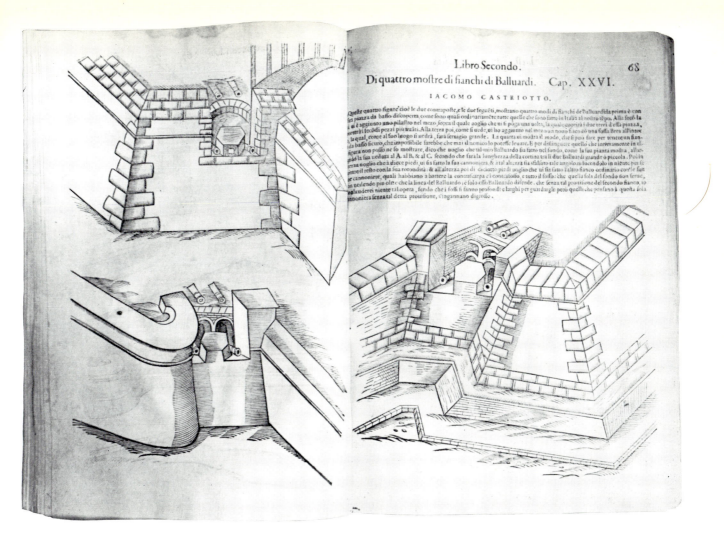

Drawings of guns firing along curtain
walls from the flanks of bastions.

Queste quattro figure cioè le due contraposte, e le due seguéti, mostrano quattro modi di fianchi de Balluardi, la prima è con sua pianza da basso discoperta, come sono quasi ordinariamére tutte quelle che sono fatte in Italia al nostro tépo. Alla seconda è aggiunto uno pilastro nel mezo sopra il quale se ui poga una uolta, la quale coprirà i due terzi d'essa piazza, nel quale resto di pezzi più uiuili. Alla terza poi, come si uede, ui ho aggiunto nel mezo una fossa per difension de i pezzi più uiuili, la qual, come al suo luogo si uedrà, farà seruigio grande. La quarta ui mostra il modo, che si può fare per uenire un fianco da basso sicuro, che impossibile sarebbe che mai il nemico lo potesse leuare. E per distinguere quello che interamente in essa figura non posso né so mostrare, dico che uoglio che tal-mio Balluardo sia fatto nel fondo, come la sua pianta mostra, allar-gato la sua uedura al A. al B. & al C. secondo che farà la lunghezza della cortina tra li due balluardi grande ò piccola. Poi in terra uoglio che à diece piedi, ui sia fatto la sua cannoniera, & à tal altezza sia sfalzato tale angolo facendolo in niéte per se stessi il resto con la sua rotondità: & all'altezza poi di diciotto piedi uoglio che ui sia fatto l'altro fianco ordinario con le sue cannoniere, quali habbiano à battere la contrascarpa e i contralotti, e tutto il fosso: che quella sola del fondo non serue, non uedendo più oltre che la linea del Balluardo: e solo esso Balluardo difende. che senza tal prouisione del secondo fianco, io uolauderei niente tal opera. sendo che i fossi si fanno profondi e larghi per guardargli però quelli che pensano è quella sola cannoniera senza tal detta prouisione, s'ingannano digrosso.

allow modern traffic to pass on each side. The middle angle is subdivided, with St Philip's bastion occupying its salient point, and supported on each side by the slightly higher bastions of St James and St Luke. At the north end, adjoining Marsamxett harbour, the angle is constructed of three bastions which terrace down towards the water's edge, and on the Grand Harbour side the salient point is occupied by a half-bastion of St Francis and the magazine bastion which faces out across the harbour. In designing the bastions the engineer had always to adjust them so that the overall length of the face of the bastion and the length of the curtain wall were well within the effective range of the defending guns placed in the flank of the adjoining bastion. It was also important that the bastions should not be acute, otherwise their salient points might easily be shot off by enemy fire. Acute-shaped bastions left very little room inside for assembling troops and artillery.

The second line of this co-ordinated defence was covered by two ravelins, more acutely angled projections, but open at the back so that if they should fall they could still be exposed to fire from the bastions and the Turks could not convert them into forts.

The front line consisted of two lunettes, open forts which could be evacuated if necessary, and which covered the re-entrant angles between the ravelins.

And finally there was a gigantic construction, a rectangular fortification thrust out on the Grand Harbour side of the defences. This was Floriani's horn-work, an envelope of stone, elaborate in construction and extensive in execution. In turn, the horn-work was protected by a crown-work, a consummate triple-pointed fortification with its own lunette fort. This is the apogee of Baroque fortification. A British officer in the Bengal Engineers described it: 'The force of outworks could no further go! Yet this whole system is itself only an advanced work to Valletta, which has its own covered way, ravelin, envelope, giant bastions and cavaliers rising in the rear.'[4]

Floriani's proposals came in for considerable criticism from the body of the Knights which necessitated a commission being appointed to study the whole picture of the defences of Valletta. This commission reported to the Grand Master in 1636, and its conclusions were in direct opposition to the proposals of Floriani. Valletta, said the Commission, was already excellently defended and only needed small additional works applying to the existing lines in order to make them impregnable. Floriani's scheme seemed too strong on the land front and too weak along its flanks facing the two harbours. The Commission then visited various engineers in diverse parts of Europe, many of whom came out in support of the Commission's report. Nevertheless, and with some reluctance, Floriani's plan was accepted and work went ahead on the chain of bastions cut from the solid rock. The engineer supervised the laying out of the trace and the initial details of the scheme, but he was in a bad temper, holding in contempt those that had opposed his plans. In deep disgust, and feeling that he had been maligned by certain persons who were envious of his renown and reputation, he left

Malta. Once more he took up his post as commander of the citadel at Ferrara and shortly afterwards died, perhaps of a broken heart, for he was only 53 years old.[5]

At this time Malta was buzzing with the activity of famous military engineers, arguing among themselves, sometimes agreeing with and sometimes disputing each other's propositions. In addition to Floriani, two other names stand out as being particularly important to the history of fortification on the island – Firenzuola and Valperga. It is to them that the main bulk of the work must be attributed. The next problem lay in finding adequate defences for the Three Cities which lay on the far side of the Grand Harbour. Vittoriosa and Senglea stood on the two narrow peninsulas, and the town of Cospicua joined them in a large half-circle. In essence the problem was threefold. The first worry was lest an enemy boat should slip into the Grand Harbour at night passing unseen the defences of Fort St Elmo. It could then create havoc among the moored vessels untouched by the guns of the fort which could not swing round to cover the Grand Harbour. Secondly, allied ships docked in the Port of Vessels were vulnerable to bombardment from the surrounding high ground. And thirdly, the existing defences of Vittoriosa and Senglea were now outdated. The posts of Castille and Auvergne, which had once been stong points, were now inadequate to meet the threat of the increased power of Turkish attack. Cospicua itself lay exposed and unprotected.

Vincenzo Masculano da Firenzuola was an Italian born in 1578. He acquired prominence and became a Dominican Cardinal and, later, Vicar General of his Order. He was a personal friend of Galileo Galilei and one of the outstanding military engineers of his day. In 1638, at the request of the Grand Master, Jean Paul Lascaris Castellar, he was invited to Malta to report on the island's fortifications.[6] On 28 September of that year he placed his proposals before the Council of the Knights, and recommended the encirclement of Cospicua with a line of open forts. Open, so that if by chance the Turks should attack and occupy them they could not be turned to good advantage and used against the Knights. This ring of bastions, first called the Margherita Lines, was later named after their designer Firenzuola. Most of these fortifications still stand, with the exception of the western bastion and curtain demolished by the British Admiralty in order to make way for an enlargement of the dockyard. Firenzuola was one of

The face of St James's bastion and the
Zabbar gate in the Cottonera Lines.

those who had criticized Floriani's designs and now in turn his project ran into adverse comment. Some said it was too expensive and the Knights could not afford this additional burden. In defence of his proposals, Firenzuola pointed out that the main cost was not in building forts but in manning them. The cost of good fortifications could be offset against the cost of running a larger garrison which would otherwise be needed to defend Malta. To and fro the argument raged. In 1640 Giovanni Medici visited Valletta and recommended the adoption of part of Firenzuola's proposals covering the front of Cospicua, but maintaining that the western line, which ran over Corradino hill, was an unnecessary extravagance.[7] Five years later Bandinelli Pallavicino added further support to the argument, pointing out that if there were another siege of Malta, the Christian princes would be unlikely to send their ships to its aid unless they could be assured of safe anchorage in the Grand Harbour and the necessary protection against long-range bombardment which the Firenzuola Lines would provide. This view was supported by the famous French engineer the Count de Pagan, so the work began.

In 1657 Lascaris died, and there followed a short period of disturbed Grand Mastership as three Knights in turn occupied the title. But in 1663 Fra Nicolas Cotoner acceded. He was a Spaniard. Of different mettle, his mind was filled with grandiose schemes and an intense desire to perpetuate his name through the creation of a monumental line of fortifications which would once and for all seal off the Three Cities from a landward attack. As a tool to immortalize his appellation, he chose the Italian military engineer Antonio Maurizio, Count of Valperga. Valperga had already written several books on the art of fortification when he arrived in Malta in the year 1670. He proposed, with the encouragement and consent of Nicolas Cotoner, the construction of a grand semicircular ring of forts stretching from the Kalkara creek at the northern edge of the town of Vittoriosa to the French creek on the western edge of Cospicua, a land line of eight regular bastions projecting between curtain walls and stretching for nearly 5000 yards. When he had arrived in February Valperga had first suggested strengthening Firenzuola's works, but this project was insufficiently magnificent to please the Grand Master, and now a mere six months later this new and grandiose scheme was prepared, augmented, and the foundation stone laid. Work on the Firenzuola Lines was suspended so that labour and capital could be

The advanced gate in the walls of Vittoriosa, 1722.

The Zejtun gate in the Cottonera Lines.

The Polverista gate and St Nicholas
curtain in the Cottonera Lines.

switched to the new fortifications. They were, as one might expect, named
after the Grand Master – the Cottonera Lines. The project received almost
universal disapproval, being considered too vast and expensive, but Cotoner
was undismayed and resolved to push on with his scheme. For ten years the
building continued with great vigour until funds ran out. The construction
of the ravelins, which it was intended should be placed between the bastions
to provide additional cover for the curtain walls, had to be abandoned. To
an onlooker the Lines are truly impressive and perhaps their magnificence
might well have deterred the Turk. But the threat of Turkish invasion was
diminishing and the power of her forces waning.

In the centre of each curtain stands a stately gateway. Alberti had once written that 'the gates should be adorned in the manner of triumphal arches,'[8] and these designs are truly triumphal. Richly modelled, heavily rusticated and adorned with the carved paraphernalia of war, they surely stand among the masterpieces of Baroque architecture in Malta. The Zabbar gate is the most splendid. Above its arch hangs the inscription recording the gift of the works by the Grand Master Nicolas Cotoner, surmounted by a bronze bust of the donor and surrounded by the rich carving of angels, spears, banners, and trumpets, the whole centrepiece raised in triumphal dedication to the man who so strongly desired his name immortalized. It was argued that Cotoner's project made the completion of the Firenzuola Lines unnecessary and was no more than an academic exercise. Nevertheless, military engineers, and among them the French designer de Tigné, were still in favour of completing the circuit in front of Cospicua. Perhaps this was understandable – it was after all their livelihood. In 1733 authority was granted for the continuation of the fortifications, and in the years that followed they were completed in a modified form.

In the Grand Harbour there remained one outstanding requirement – the need to seal the harbour mouth. In 1670 work began on the construction of Fort Ricasoli to the designs of Valperga. Built opposite St Elmo, it occupied the whole of the promontory – a longitudinal fort whose curtain and bastions rose from the water's edge and whose land front was protected by three powerful bastions from which thrust forward two long pointed ravelins. It therefore assumes the form of a crown-work. Its fine Baroque gateway, with spiral columns, looks out across the water of Kalkara creek. The gate was severely damaged in the air blitz of 1941, but has since been inaccurately restored.

The engineer Valperga also drew up the plans for the suburb of Floriana, which was named in honour of his compatriot – perhaps some recompense for the abuse Floriani received during his visit to Malta. The design of Floriana was carefully considered. No houses were permitted to have cellars, and the heights of all building were carefully controlled so that the guns on the ramparts of Valletta could cover them in the event of their being captured by the Turks. The city streets were laid out in a regular geometrical pattern so that they could be enfiladed by the Valletta guns.[9]

The defence of the Grand Harbour was now secured – on the Valletta side by the extension of the land front to Floriana and before the Three

Cities by five lines of fortification: the inner citadel of Fort St Angelo which was separated from the mainland by a strip of water cut to provide safe berth for the galleys of the Order during the great siege of 1565; the old land fronts of Vittoriosa and Senglea strengthened and rebuilt after the siege; the Firenzuola Lines circling Cospicua; the Cottonera Lines embracing the whole group of towns; and, to seaward, Fort Ricasoli.

Precautions now were needed against a possible attack across the waters of Marsamxett, where the northern flank of Valletta and Floriana was exposed to bombardment and where the sole deterrent to penetration into this harbour rested upon the effectiveness of the guns on Fort St Elmo. As early as the sixteenth century the island which lay undefended in the harbour of Marsamxett was noted as a possible source of danger and it was proposed to erect a fort there, but this was low on the list of priorities, for time was short and money scarce. In late January 1681 Don Carlos de Grunenberg, military engineer to the King of Spain in Sicily, arrived in Malta. He took up the theme of the undefended flank of Valletta and reiterated the proposal for constructing a fort on the island. Once again the pressure of their other commitments caused the Knights to shelve this solution. The Floriana Lines had cost a fortune and the even larger project of Nicolas Cotoner had drained the exchequer. Meanwhile, Grunenberg prepared a series of stone scale models for new gun batteries at forts Ricasoli, St Elmo, St Angelo and St Michael, and these fascinating models are still preserved in the Valletta armoury. In the case of the model of Fort St Angelo a section can be removed showing an alternative scheme, and Grunenberg's proposals are tinted yellow. He advocated building fausse-braie. These are batteries constructed practically at water level so that their guns can sweep the surface of the harbours and, at close range, bring devastating power to bear on any attacking vessels.

In the early years of the eighteenth century, the project for fortifying the island in Marsamxett was revived by the Grand Master, Ramon Perellos, who called two engineers to Malta, but there was further delay and the building was not commissioned until a Portuguese Knight, Don Antonio de Vilhena, assumed the Grand Mastership in 1722. Fort Manoel is the classic example of a Baroque fortress – bold yet precise, elegant yet a hard functional machine. It was designed by de Tigné working in the manner of the French school which, by this time, had assumed leadership in the art

An early drawing of Fort Manoel
showing the demi-lune battery far out in
front, and the lunette halfway between
the battery and the fort. These two
features were not built.

of fortification. The fortress was modelled on the work of Vauban, that
master of theory and technique whose name still survives above all others
in the field.

Throughout the seventeenth century the Turks had been active and the
Knights could not afford to rest on their laurels. In 1641 a raiding force of
about 5000 soldiers had landed at Marsaskala bay, but had been checked
and driven off by a strong force of Maltese cavalry. A little later sixty Turkish galleys appeared off the coast near Marsaxlokk, but were discouraged
from putting men ashore by the guns of Fort St Lucian. In 1645 there was
another threat of invasion, but attention was shifted to the Venetian islands
against whom the Turks declared war. The Morea was recaptured and the

Venetian fortresses on the island of Crete once more fell to Ottoman forces. In 1672 they captured Lemberg and Lublin in Poland and nine years later their forces battered on the gates of Vienna, which was seriously menaced until relieved by the timely arrival of Jan Sobieski's army. More and more, Turkish eyes were turning to the north east as the pressure against Russia grew.

The new fortress was named after the Portuguese Grand Master. Fort Manoel is a square fort with its strongest front facing north. Originally de Tigné intended covering the whole of Manoel island with fortifications and projecting on this northern front a battery far out in front to take the initial shock of any attack. Halfway between this battery and the main fort he proposed a lunette which would give supporting fire to the forward guns and provide a staging point for troops which might have to be withdrawn from the advanced battery. Fort Manoel is a beautiful essay in strict geometry, incorporating all the refinements of Vauban's engineering. Four corner bastions are separated from the surrounding terrain by a wide ditch and reinforced on the north front by a ravelin, a triangular strong-point covering the curtain wall. Between the ravelin and the curtain lies a tenaille and caponiere. The tenaille is dug into the ditch and provides a space for soldiers with muskets to cover the back of the ravelin and the ditch on each side. The caponiere is a trench, protected by parapets, so that soldiers could move unhindered between the projecting ravelin and the main body of the fort. Beyond the ditch there is a covered way surrounding the fortress. This is termed 'covered' because it is protected from the view of the enemy by a raised parapet. At regular intervals along the covered way depressions are made, called places of arms, where soldiers could be assembled, either to break out for a counter-attack, or to withstand a sudden attack from any particular quarter. Beyond these, stretching out like long pointed fingers, lie the glacis, smooth surfaces of stone, the angles adjusted so that guns on the parapet could pour devastating fire on to any enemy who should venture that far. A comparison between Fort Manoel and the sixteenth-century, star-shaped fort of St Elmo will show the remarkable development in the art of fortification. At St Elmo the bastions are acute, long-pointed and the curtain walls short, or non-existent. At Manoel the curtain walls are increased in size in order to provide maximum accommodation inside the fort itself, but the curtains are covered by ravelins which stand clear of the main work like separate fortresses. The trace has become far more complicated and the adjustment of each angle and the length of each piece more precisely determined, calling for an increased knowledge of mathematics on the part of the military engineers. These men could not resist the opportunity for elaborate architectural embellishment.

The main gate at Manoel is a magnificent Baroque design, richly carved and deeply cut. The buildings of the fort are fine proportioned structures -- a chapel and barracks all built to the highest standards. In spite of a direct hit in the air bombardment of the last war, Fort Manoel still retains its overall shape and pattern – a fitting monument to the fortress builders of Malta.

The northern gap was finally closed and the harbour of Marsamxett sealed from the enemy by the constructions of yet another fort, Fort Tigné on the promontory opposite St Elmo. Its name was taken, not from the French military engineer who had designed Fort Manoel, but from Chevalier Tigné who, in 1792, at the expense of the Grand Master de Rohan, designed and built this small casemated fort. It is an advanced bastion whose sole duty is to assist the garrison of Fort St Elmo in protecting the mouth of Marsamxett harbour. It was the last important defence post to be constructed by the Order before its capitulation to Napoleon's troops.

The original strategy of the Knights of St John was based upon the concept of defending the Grand Harbour and its creeks. It will be seen how the major defensive systems were designed to encircle, first the old town of Il Borgo and the castle of St Angelo then, with the building of Valletta, lines spread out in a great circle providing defence in depth for the waters of both the Grand Harbour and Marsamxett, with the new capital of Valletta sitting snugly in their centre. The villages which the Knights found on Malta, and those which later grew, were left to their own undefended devices, to be sacrificed to an invading force if needs be. Only the two old capitals, Mdina in Malta and Rabat in Gozo, had encircling walls of fortifications which, if not very powerful, were assisted by the elevated position of the towns. The citadel at Rabat provided a refuge for the Gozitan farmers. The fortified town of Mdina proved its worth in the Great Siege of 1565 when it became an acute embarrassment to the Turkish general.

The building of a new fortified town, Fort Chambray, at the landing stage in Gozo was contemplated only towards the end of the Knights' occupation of Malta. The defences were built, but the project was not fully realized.

The fine Baroque gateway to Fort
Manoel.

Outlying fortified towers were built to watch for Turkish invasion. This is the Qawra tower on the rocky coast of Gozo.

The Knights appreciated the inadequacy of their garrison and the long perimeter of the coast line of the two islands, and until the mid-eighteenth century they made no attempt to prevent a large-scale Turkish landing on Malta. The most they could ever hope to do was to hang on behind their strong lines of defence until a relief force could be assembled in Sicily and sent to their aid. However, the defences of Valletta and the Three Cities were supplemented in two ways. Firstly by constructing a number of watch towers sufficiently strong to resist musket fire and the sudden attack by small parties of marauders, but incapable of withstanding a long siege. These towers were constructed mainly round the coast line and could signal to each other in the event of danger. Bonfires were lit on their flat roofs as a

The forbidding Red tower on the crest of the Marfa ridge.

warning of invasion and an elaborate signalling system was devised. This was primarily intended for signalling from ship to shore and consisted of various combinations of gunfire and flags.[10] Since earliest times watch towers have been built in Malta, but those now standing date from the occupation of the Knights of St John and the Allied armed forces of the last war. Some were designed to watch inlets or vulnerable landing places and, consequently, they had to dominate the view; some formed a refuge for the villagers against the attack of corsairs, as for example the tower built in 1727 at Mqabba; and some were built as lookout towers to dominate other lower lines of defence. It was from a tower like this, the Torre dell'Orologio at Vittoriosa, that the Grand Master la Valette conducted the defence during the siege of 1565 and was able to obtain information of the disposition of the Turkish forces. This was an old Siculo-Norman tower of six floors modified by the Knights in 1549.[11] It was destroyed in the second world war.

The coastal look-out towers varied in size. The small ones normally consisted of a single room on each floor reached by a ladder. The base of the building was constructed of thick stone walls built sloping inwards and the roof usually had crenellation to protect the spotters. Decoration was confined to a roll moulding at the top of the sloping base and sometimes to carved escutcheon over the doorway.[12] The Red tower at Mellieha, built in 1649, is one of the most impressive examples, standing gaunt on the last ridge before the Comino channel. Its base, some twelve feet high, slopes out sharply from a bold torus moulding at main floor level. The doorway is approached by a flight of stone steps and was probably originally separated by a small drawbridge. The interior consists of one floor with a double barrel-vaulted ceiling, providing a space about thirty yards square, and its outer walls are nearly fourteen feet thick. Through these walls small windows are cut and in one corner a stone spiral staircase rises to the flat roof. The roof has a two-foot parapet and four corner towers rising a further ten feet into the air. This is a miniature fortress.

Secondly, a number of small forts were constructed at vulnerable points to fire on to bays and likely landing points. These forts were large enough to protect a small garrison, and sufficiently strong to encourage the enemy to by-pass them rather than waste time on their destruction. Gerolomo Cassar's son, Vittorio, built the splendidly powerful fort on Comino in 1618, which commanded the two channels between Gozo and Malta. Square,

Fort St Lucian constructed in 1610, by Vittorio, the son of Gerolamo Cassar.

Drawbridge and moat at St Thomas's fort.

robust in shape, its base rises vertically to a string moulding upon which were constructed the four corner towers. Between them curtain walls cut back and rise to the same overall height. About this time two impressive isolated forts were built in the land south of the Grand Harbour. Fort St Lucian, constructed in 1610, looks out over the wide bay of Marsaxlokk, that vulnerable inlet where the Turkish troops landed in 1565. The fort is a square block of impressive bulk rising above a wide ditch. It appears to have had a drawbridge and portcullis. The design is somewhat similar to the Comino fort in that the curtain walls are sloping, but in this case they merely extend the sloping face of the basement storey. Fort St Thomas commands the entrance to Marsaskala creek and the wide bay of St Thomas. It is a square fort with four corner bastions, portcullis and drawbridge. Its gaunt appearance must have had a deterrent effect and somewhat appropriately it was used as army detention barracks in the second world war.

The strong fort of St Thomas guarded the waters of Marsaskala and St Thomas's bay. It was built in 1614.

Only by the mid-eighteenth century did the Knights feel sufficiently confident to face the enemy on the beaches. By this time an effective Maltese militia had been recruited and trained, and plans were drawn up for encircling the perimeters of Malta and Gozo with a ring of stone. Where the cliffs were steep and unscalable the natural rock was sufficient defence in itself, but where the ground sloped gently to a sandy bay or rocky coast, defensive walls were to be constructed linking the existing towns and forts to new stone redoubts. Only part of this grand project was realized.

Finally, there was the partially defended house providing limited protection against small bands of rangers. These varied in scale from the small farm with its fortified tower, in which the farmer and his family could take

A tower built to defend a farmhouse near Marsaskala.

The Grand Master's palace at Verdala,
designed by Gerolamo Cassar and begun
in 1586.

refute, to stately piles, such as the Verdala palace. The problem was how to provide the delights of the country villa's relaxation, the relief from pomp and circumstance, the pleasure of shady groves of trees, in fact, all the benefits derived from living in the country, without the attendant dangers of residence outside the fortified walls of a citadel? The Grand Master and his associates needed a break from the civic responsibilities of the head-quarters, and the semi-fortified villa provided the answer. What a prize the kidnapping of the Grand Master would have been to the Turks! At Verdala, not far from Mdina and beyond the last houses of Rabat, the Grand Master, Fra Hughes de Verdale, built for himself a summer palace on high ground to attract the blessings of the cool summer breezes. It stands amidst the dark green leaves of the Boschetto. The architect was Gerolamo Cassar and work began in the year 1586. Half fort, half villa, the building is modelled on the Villa Farnese at Caprarola, but without the central circular room. Cassar may well have seen that villa when he visited Rome, for he was certainly conversant with the architecture of Vignola. Four thin corner bastions are reminiscent of military architecture, and their faces are lined up so that they could be covered by musketry fire from portholes in the opposite flanks. But the villa could not have withstood a siege, nor a violent assault, and the bastions act more as symbols of a military heritage, fitting attributes to the residence of the Grand Master of the Knights.

There are numerous examples in Europe of country houses which retain the trappings of military architecture where already the threat of attack had passed – a kind of sop to tradition. Moat, drawbridge, bastions might all have been necessary for the residence of the Grand Master, but could hardly be justified on practical grounds in the eighteenth century.

Selmun palace, which stands on the high ground beyond St Paul's bay, is a building obviously inspired by the Verdala palace, but is richer, cruder and more ornate. Both in plan and elevation there are similarities with Cassar's palace. The Selmun palace was designed by the Maltese architect Giuseppe Cachia. It is said that the building was originally built as an institution for the redemption of slaves, but from its design it seems ideally intended as a country villa and was doubtless used for this purpose. The ground floor has a sloping base and yet contains the main entrance. The first floor assumes the character of the piano nobile and is completely surrounded with an external balcony on to which give generous moulded windows. The

The Selmun palace, a villa designed by Giuseppe Cachia in the eighteenth century.

ground around the palace was excellent shooting country and in 1649 part of it and the adjoining islet were granted to the Knight Miguell Torrellos y Semenat, Prior of Catalonia, as a preserve for rabbit shooting. The building now serves as a gracious country hotel, an adaptation in sympathy with its original use as a country villa.

The main garrisons for defence were concentrated in the cities. In 1716 it was estimated that 8000 infantry and 150 cavalry were stationed in Valletta and Floriana, of whom 3000 were regular troops and 5000 militia. A similar number were stationed in the Three Cities to defend the Cotton-era and Firenzuola Lines and 2000 garrisoned at Fort Ricasoli to guard the Grand Harbour mouth. Not a very large force when one considers the strategic importance of Malta, and only feasible when one considers the immense power of resistance of the stone fortifications which the Knights had heaped up to their aid.[13]

[1] Floriani (Pompeii). *Discorso intorno all' isola di Malta e di cio ché potrà succedere tentando il Turco tal impresa, ecc.* (Macerata 1576).

[2] Floriani (Pietro Paolo). *Difese et Ofesa delle piazze di P.P.F., Opera non solo utile e necessaria a capitani e governatori di fortezza, manco di sommo profitto a studiosi dell'historia militari così antichi come moderne* (Macerata 1630). Second edition (Venice 1654). Second part of title added for new edition.

[3] Archives of Malta – *Parere e considerazione sopra le fortificazioni della Città di Valletta, e sopra il sito da edificarsi per il sign. Pietro Paolo Floriani, 1632.*

[4] Yule (Henry). *Fortification for officers of the army and students of Military History* (London 1851), page 11 g.

[5] Much of the biography of Floriani is taken from Clausetti (Enrico). 'Pietro Paolo Floriani, ingegnere militare 1585–1638' in *Palladio – Rivista di storia dell'architettura*, Volume 3, No.1 (1939).

[6] For details see the articles on the 'Firenzuola Lines' by Paul Galea in *Sunday Times of Malta* (3 June, 10 June, 24 June and 1 July 1956).

[7] Vatican Library. MSS. Chigiani N.III 61, page 71.

[8] Alberti (Leon Battista). *Ten Books of Architecture* translated by James Leoni (London 1755), Book VIII, chapter vi, page 172.

[9] Mifsud (A.). *Knights Hospitalers*, page 296.

[10] I am indebted to Roger di Giorgio for showing me a coloured manuscript of these signals.

[11] Mifsud (A.). 'La milizia e le torri antiche di Malta' in *Archivum Melitense*, Volume 4, No.2 (1920), pages 55–100.

[12] *Op. cit.*, page 302.

[13] Crocker (J.) *History of the Fortifications of Malta* (Malta 1920), page 14. Information taken from a French manuscript in the office of the Chief Engineer of the British Garrison.

Chapter 6: The Old Capital

Mdina lies high on the middle ledge which runs along the south-western edge of the island, sloping gently to the ports and inundations on the north-eastern seaboard. Malta is a tilted shelf with high precipitous cliffs on one side, the shelf dipping gently to the shallow sea on the other. Mdina, at 500 feet, is in a commanding position and has been occupied from earliest times. The original capital of Malta, it was called Melita by the Greeks, a name synonymous with the island itself. The seat of the Roman Governor Publius, who received St Paul with such hospitality, it was fortified by the Arabs, its walls extending beyond those standing today. An early and admittedly inaccurate map does show the whole town encircled by walls and towers which follow the sheer edge of the cliff except across the southern front where the ridge continues towards what is now Verdala, and had to be excavated to form a defensive moat. There are twenty-six towers and two main approaches bridging the moat. A smaller gate stands on the eastern perimeter to act as a sally port leading down the steep cliff face. The drawing depicts a medieval system of defence without bastions, the closely spaced towers being connected by lengths of curtain wall. The Arabs called the place Mdina, and its suburb Rabat.

The Normans arrived in 1090 and built there a Romanesque cathedral with a free-standing bell tower. The cathedral occupied the site of a small ruined sanctuary which in turn had been built where once stood the house of Publius, who, after conversion and baptism at the hands of St Paul, became the first bishop of Malta. So the city has a long and noble history. In 1422 the city was attacked by a considerable force of some 18,000 Turkish soldiers operating from the Barbary coast. Although they laid waste most of the island of Malta they did not penetrate the capital. It is reputed that the Maltese defenders were given new heart by the timely arrival of an apparition of St Paul mounted on a white charger and brandishing an enormous sword. This was fortunate as the fortifications could not have been all that strong. In 1427 it was christened Città Notabile by King Alfonso of Aragon in recognition of the services of its Maltese citizens.

When the Knights arrived, the Grand Master, Philippe Villiers de l'Isle Adam visited Notabile, but chose for his headquarters the little port of Il Borgo. During the Great Siege, Notabile assumed an active role in the rear of the Turkish lines; its cavalry was largely responsible for turning the tide

The walls of Mdina and the dome of its cathedral dominate the skyline of the island.

of war when it suddenly attacked the Turkish base-camp and caused Mustapha Pasha to pull back his main forces when victory seemed in their hands.

Prior to the siege, the walls of Notabile had been strengthened by the Knights and two bastions constructed on the extremities of the land front. Perez Aleccio's scene of the withdrawal of the Turkish forces depicts a very inaccurate Notabile surrounded by a ditch, but it does show the two land bastions and the old Romanesque cathedral which was later destroyed by an earthquake. Elsewhere, Aleccio depicts an accurate plan of the defences of Notabile overlaid with a suggestion for reducing the perimeter of the city, and constructing two powerful bastions facing south, a new central gate entering the town through the curtain between these bastions, and covered by a small ravelin. Fortunately, these defences were never built for they would have entailed the destruction of many of the fine old buildings which still survive in the city. With the subsequent construction of Valletta and the removal of the headquarters of the Knights from Il Borgo to that new

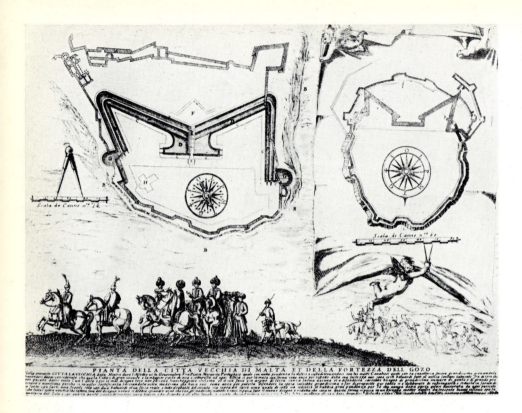

Perez Aleccio's drawing shows the proposal to build a new and shorter perimeter for the defence of Mdina. Fortunately these defences were never built for they would have entailed the destruction of many of the fine old buildings which still survive in the city.

capital, Notabile became known as the old city – Città Vecchia. Only in modern times has it reverted to its Arab name, Mdina. In 1645 there was feverish activity in Malta as defence works were pushed ahead to thwart an impending Turkish attack. Notable military engineers recommended concentration on the task of implementing the defences of Valletta and the Three Cities. Some considered that Notabile was indefensible and that, rather than allow it to fall into Turkish hands and so give them a fine, well-stocked base camp, its defensive walls should be pulled down and its guns removed. This proposal led to serious rioting in the city and had to be cancelled. Fortunately the pressure was released when in that year the Turks shifted their attention to the island of Crete, which they attacked with great ferocity.

An accurate plan drawn in 1724 shows the land front reinforced by a large central bastion and another bastion constructed behind the cathedral above the steep cliff face. Of the three old gates, two still remain, but the

The triumphal main gateway into the
old capital built in 1724.

third was blocked when a new triumphal archway was constructed in that year, approached by a drawbridge over the moat. This is a fine Baroque design consisting of rusticated pillars and rich carving surmounted by an ornate superstructure – a fitting triumphal entry to the old city. Inside, a small square was formed, flanked on one side by the old Signal Tower of the Standard, which pre-dates the arrival of the Knights but was modernized by them. Facing the tower stands the Magisterial palace, a late work of one of the best Maltese architects, Giovanni Barbara. Although he studied in Rome, there seems to be here an influence from France. The richly carved main door is faintly suggestive, with its banded columns, of the work of Philibert de l'Orme. French too are the segmental-headed windows which mark the basement on each side of the main door, and the plan, an open courtyard with the palace set back around three sides of it and a screen occupying the fourth side, is reminiscent of many Parisian palaces. The Magisterial palace was probably designed in 1730, the year that Barbara died. Also in Mdina, close to the cathedral, Barbara designed the fine Baroque seminary which was built in 1733. This is quite different, and much more Italian in flavour. On each side of the main door, powerful torsos support the entablature at the first floor balcony. So different is the character that it is difficult to believe that the two buildings are by the same architect.

On the third side of the square facing the town gate stands the nunnery of St Benedict. It dates from 1418, but most of the exterior was built in the seventeenth century. The nunnery still adheres to strict rules; the only men being permitted to enter are the doctor and the whitewasher. This is a stark, forbidding building, both as a recluse and an architectural closure for the little square. Its small, high-placed windows and severe plain walls remind us of the words of Alberti written in the same century as the founding of this nunnery: 'It is our Business in both to take Care not that they have no Inclinations to be unchaste, but no Means. For this Purpose every Entrance must be so secured, that nobody can possibly get in; and so well watched, that nobody may loyter about in order to attempt it without instant Suspicion and Shame. No Camp for an Army should be so well guarded by Intrenchments and Palisades, as a Monastery ought to be by high Walls, without either Doors or Windows in them, or the least Hole by which not only no Violator of Chastity, but not so much as the least Temptation either by Eye or Ear, may possibly get in to disorder, and pollute the Minds of the

Giovanni Barbara's Magisterial palace at Mdina shows French Baroque influence.

Left: The Tower of the Standards remodelled by the Knights.

Right: The Santa Sophia palace, a Siculo-Norman building in Mdina.

The Norman house.

Lorenzo Gafà's dynamic dome on the cathedral.

Overleaf, page 160:
Mattia Preti's painting in the choir of the cathedral shows 'The shipwreck of St Paul'.

Overleaf, page 161:
The façade of the cathedral.

Recluse.'[1] A hundred years later Catanio reinforced Alberti's argument. 'In ancient times', he wrote, 'it was a habit to build convents and nunneries outside the town walls. This should not be done at all, because in time of war the convent can be very useful to the enemy . . .'[2]

Some of the oldest palaces still stand in Mdina. In style they are termed Siculo-Norman, something of a misnomer as they nearly all date from the period of Aragonese occupation. These are town houses built around internal courtyards which contain a stone staircase. The buildings are modest in scale, and the exterior severe with only limited decoration. The lower parts of the buildings look strong, built for limited defence and punctuated only occasionally by plain Gothic doorways. These unpretentious palaces are an amalgam of foreign styles, though not unnaturally most strongly

Sunlight on colour-washed stone: the base of a cathedral column.

influenced from nearby Sicily. We can see this in the shape of the miniature arcading used as a string course at first-floor levels and the small decorated Gothic windows on the upper floors.[3] Some of these palaces go back in date to the thirteenth century but most of what remains is fifteenth century with considerable modifications carried out on buildings such as the Norman house after the advent of the Knights in 1530. In those years many buildings, which had previously been single storey, had additional rooms built upstairs. They are now quiet and dignified, although most are still occupied and well preserved by the ancient families of Malta, filled with the art treasures like veritable museums.

Both by day and by night the city is very quiet, few cars disturb the peace of its narrow, twisting streets and pedestrians seem compelled to observe a sober silence. At night the real serene beauty of the city is apparent, as the street lights cast warm pools of light on the cream stone surfaces of the walls and pavements. Mdina has a remarkable unity preserved intact from another generation.

The cathedral dominates all other buildings. It is the most important work of the Maltese architect Lorenzo Gafà, and probably the finest domed church on the island. Lorenzo was sent to Rome by the Knights, where his brother Melchiore was already making a name for himself as a sculptor. Lorenzo Gafà arrived there about 1700 to study the latest style of architec-

The side walls of the Archbishop's palace at Mdina are panelled in the manner of late seventeenth-century work in Rome.

ture, and he soon fell under the spell of Francesco Borromini, that most original of Roman Baroque architects and master of dome construction. His St Agnese dome in the Piazza Navona must have had a profound effect upon Lorenzo, starting him on a career in Malta, the result of which was the erection of a number of splendid domed churches. The largest and the most impressive is the cathedral at Mdina. The old Norman basilica, together with many other buildings on the island, was destroyed in the devastating earthquake of 1693, when in Sicily the town of Catania was practically wiped out. The Mdina dome is Gafà's masterpiece; much bolder and more dynamic than anything he has attempted before, Gafà mounts great moulding scrolls on the dome and brings forward the eight corners of the octagon with serried rows of coupled pilasters. This dome and the rich interior are near the summit of Baroque art and, unlike the conventual church in Valletta, the work is all of one period. It was completed in five years, and the building consecrated in 1702. It had been an expensive venture, which involved not only the construction of this large church but the purchase and clearing of buildings in front so that it might face an adequate piazza. During demolition work in front of the cathedral in April 1698, workmen discovered under the floor of one of the houses a vase full of gold pieces. All exclaimed 'this is a miracle of St Paul wrought to provide for the completion of the temple', but there was a dispute about the use to which the money should be put, and an appeal had to be made to Innocent XII. He ruled that half should go towards the fabric of the church, and half put in trust. Lorenzo Gafà refused payment for his work, so it was resolved to give him an annual funeral celebration in perpetuity after his death – a grateful recognition of his services to Malta.[4]

When the French troops under Napoleon occupied the island and made themselves so unpopular, the event which sparked off the Maltese revolt took place in Mdina. Captain Masson, Commander of the French garrison in Mdina, was thrown from a window in Notary Bezzina's house in Villagaignon street and killed by the infuriated populace. This was in 1798, and it signalled the final assault on the citadel. The Maltese stormed it from two sides, the main body attacking from the suburb, Rabat, and a practically unarmed group, climbing the steep cliff face and the de Redin bastion behind the cathedral, caught the French garrison between the two fires and practically annihilated them.

The skyline of the old city.

Now the city is quiet, its dignified buildings preserved and its architectural atmosphere intact. Alterations are discouraged, and unsuitable additions prohibited so that it remains one of the most perfect examples of the past in Europe.[5]

[1] Alberti (Leon Battista). *De re aedificatoria* (Rome 1485), Book V, chapter vii. English translation by James Leoni (London 1726).

[2] Cataneo (Pietro). *I quattro primi libri di architettura* (Venice 1554). Book I, chapter vi, page 8r.

[3] For an excellent study of these and other early buildings in Malta see Perkins (J. Ward). 'Medieval and Early Renaissance Architecture in Malta' in *Antiquaries Journal*, Volume 22 (1942).

[4] Ciantar (Gio. Antonio). *Malta Illustrata*, (Malta 1780), Volume 2, page 94.

[5] Sammut (Edward). *The Monuments of Mdina* (Malta 1960) contains a full and accurate description of the city and its art treasures.

Chapter 7: The Country Parishes

The population of Malta and Gozo was sparse before the arrival of the Knights of St John in 1530. It was concentrated in the two hill-top citadels and clustered in the small village of Il Borgo which faced on to the waters of the Grand Harbour. Elsewhere farmers lived in the open countryside, and a few small hamlets stood mainly in the south of the island of Malta. Few churches existed and these mainly troglodyte. Cut into the living rock, they were safer from spying eyes and raiding corsairs than normal buildings. The few country churches were simple, plain rectangles enclosing a single cell, often almost square in shape. When in 1436 the parishes were re-organized into ten, a number of these small churches were built. The little church of Our Lady of Victory at Ta Kali is typical, and so also is the church of St Dominica at Zabbar where a remarkable early fresco has been discovered. This depicts Our Lady of Graces, supported by Saint Dominica and Saint Catherine of Alexandra.[1] The original fresco was painted in white, yellow, red, and black, and was obviously inspired by contemporary work in Italy. The Zabbar church consisted of one room measuring seventeen feet wide and twenty-one feet long, its length sub-divided by two gothic arches supporting the stone slabs of the roof. The shallow pitched roof, which extended to the end elevations, gave them a rudimentary shape not dissimilar from a classical temple. The doorway was a plain gothic-shaped arch. Above this a small rectangular window was inserted, surmounted by a bell tower of a later date, probably sixteenth century. Each side of the doorway, high up on the wall, were placed two flag poles. Rain water was thrown clear of the building by means of two water spouts, representing

The interior of the ruined chapel of St Cecilia in Gozo shows the typical method of Maltese roof construction.

cannons, on each side wall.

The church of Ta Bir Miftuh, near Gudja, is of the same period and is very similar in style. The pitch of the roof here is hidden behind the low parapet wall which gives the building a box-like shape. Larger than the other two, this church has five water spouts on each side wall and a more elaborate bell tower which was added in 1578. In front of the church is a terrace which forms part of the consecrated ground and acted at one time as a sanctuary. The present terrace was rebuilt in the late nineteenth century. Ta Bir Miftuh was the parish church for a group of hamlets which later developed and outgrew their church. As the villages expanded they called for independence and in 1592 Tarxien was disjoined, in 1634 Luqa

The façade of St Mary 'Ta Bir Miftuh', the old parish church at Gudja, was built in 1436, but the bell tower was added much later.

became a separate parish, and in 1656 Gudja itself built a new parish church so that Ta Bir Miftuh became superfluous.[2]

The Knights brought prosperity and soon after they arrived the population began to increase so that new villages sprang up and old ones expanded. The map made by Jean Quentin in 1536 shows very few villages, and those are concentrated in the south-east of Malta, whereas the map made by Lafrery in 1551 shows some thirty villages well established even before the Great Siege. Not only did the Knights bring with them a prospect of security, they also imported a modicum of classical taste from the mainland of Italy. A certain elegance and grace now becomes evident in the building of the small, simple, rectangular churches. Fifteenth-century examples were often

The Gothic vaulting in St Gregory at
Zejtun is unusual in Malta.

The small church of St Gregory at
Zejtun dates from the fifteenth century,
but the charming Renaissance doorway
was added after the arrival of the Knights
in 1530.

Overleaf, page 172:
St Gregory at Zejtun. The north wall of
the nave.

Overleaf, page 173:
Our Lady of Sorrows at Pietà, built in
1590, with a Baroque doorway added
later.

modernized and extended. St Gregory at Zejtun has transepts and a shallow saucer dome placed across the east end of the old church, the scale of the new part being considerably greater than that of its predecessor. An unusual feature for Malta is the transepts roofed with quadripartite Gothic vaults. Also the plain stone walls of the transepts are externally buttressed and supported by a battered base which has all the appearance of a work of fortification. A small bell tower and a charming renaissance doorway were added to the west front.

At Pietà in 1590 Our Lady of Sorrows was built, and in the seventeenth century it was embellished with sculpture and a rich Baroque portal.

The island abounds in these small churches. In essentials they are similar, varying only in their details. Tal Ingrau at Zejtun is the simplest possible statement, yet it is precise, confident, and beautifully proportioned. St

The chapel of the 'Tal Ingrau' near Zejtun, built in 1597.

St Roque at Balzan was built in 1593.

Roque at Balzan, on the other hand, is elegant – almost sophisticated, with its moulded pediment, decorated door, and carved window piece. St Roque at Zebbug is naïve and yet eminently successful as a result of great simplicity. The pediment moulding is slightly tilted at the corners. The window above the door has become an eye, its mouldings projected forward to catch the sun and to throw a glancing shadow across the façade. The bell tower is thin and graceful, and a diminutive forecourt acts as an atrium. St Peter at Qormi is more elaborate. Two plain pilasters define the edges of the main façade and the pediment moulding flattens out to cap them. Spouts like cannons jut from near the tops of the pilasters. The doorway is elegant Renaissance, carved by a sculptor with some classical training.

St Roque at Zebbug with its small atrium in which refugees could gain asylum.

St Peter at Qormi.

The Baroque chapel of St Peter at Lija
continues the tradition of the early
Maltese chapels.

'Zeus and Hera'. A doorknocker in Villagaignon street at Mdina.

Overleaf, page 180:
The parish church of St Philip at Zebbug (1599).

Overleaf, page 181:
At Tarxien parish church the towers began to be enveloped by a later development which was not completed.

St Catherine 'Tat Torba' is the strangest variation on the theme. In 1662 a new façade was added as a screen, practically obscuring the plain church behind. Its skyline pierced by carving and mock battlements, this screen is divided into rectangular panels in order to bring an element of recession into the treatment of the façade. It is cubic, bulky, almost heavy-handed and an extreme contrast to the very delicately carved mouldings of the canopy and the slightly splayed opening of the doorway.[3]

Meanwhile the villages began to grow in size and importance. The new city of Valletta had expanded so rapidly in the beginning that it tended to drain off population from the surrounding countryside, in particular from the Three Cities, but soon all the urban areas slowly revived. The harbour towns were well placed to participate in the naval and commercial activities of the Knights and were protected from attack by fortifications. Prosperity spread like ripples on a pool, extending to the outermost villages, increasing the demand for houses.

In order to relieve this pressure, a new town called Paola was established on the high ground to the south-west of the Three Cities, at the instigation of the Grand Master Antoine de Paule. Unlike the traditional Maltese villages, it is laid out on a grid plan. Cleverly sited longitudinal streets, lined up on the cavaliers of the Valletta fortifications, and transverse streets point directly on to the dome of Mdina cathedral. Gone was any suggestion of Laparelli's 'pleasant and sweet serpentine way'; the Order of St John was now committed to the European practice of the quadrilateral town plan. From the time of Vitruvius, Roman writer and theoretician, town planners had been absorbed with the problem of designing their cities in relation to the direction of the winds. At Paola the alignment is adjusted in such a way that the main streets run from the north-north-west in order that the town, built on the crest of the hill, could attract the cool, healthy breezes from that quarter. Nevertheless, the town was not a success, and few people opted to move out from the protection of the fortifications which girdled Valletta and the Three Cities. The Order planned extensions to Qormi and other villages, but a disastrous plague in 1676 reduced the island's population, considerably easing the pressure on housing.

The other villages grew slowly, and until recently they have remained comparatively compact. Each presents a tortuous maze of streets and houses huddled together, plain buildings facing directly onto the street from which

their doors are separated only by a step. There are no pavements, just the horizontal surface of the road and the sheer rising walls of the buildings. Behind their plain exteriors often lie surprises. Pleasant courtyards abound, cooled and ornamented by luxurious climbing plants, vine, oleander, palm, and fig. The plain façades of the houses give no indication of the scale of their interiors. These often contain richly decorated rooms, painted ceilings, carved stone door frames and priceless works of art. Here is the remnant of a Greek tradition where the citizen makes no external boast of his possessions.

The tortuous pattern of the streets allows the possibility of a surprise around each corner. Shafts of sunlight strike and illuminate a wall surface,

Left: A seventeenth-century balcony on a house at Tarxien.

Right: The façade of the parish church of St George at Qormi.

deep shade contrasts where the buildings are lit only by reflected light. At best the buildings are uniform in colour, warm stone or cream washed to prevent the splashing rain spoiling the surface. The openings are unmoulded holes in plain wall surfaces closed in the heat of the day by shuttered windows and simple boarded doors. Everywhere there are splendid heavy brass door knockers, dolphins, nymphs, mermaids, and a host of variations. Contrast is provided by the change of direction in the streets, variations in the sizes of the frontages and the heights of the roofs. All the private buildings are rectangular, flat roofed, giving a geometrical cohesion to the villages, interrupted and highlighted by the churches designed to provide necessary contrast.

The façade of Dingli's parish church of
St Mary at Attard (1613).

The façade of the parish church at
Birkirkara was designed by Tommaso
Dingli; the tower and much of the now
damaged interior are by Vittorio Cassar.

185

Each village is dominated by its large parish church crowned by a high generous dome on a monumental drum. Each church differs so that from a distance it is easy to identify the villages of Malta. The parish churches usually have two towers placed either adjacent to the west front, or close to the transepts. In Naxxar, for instance, there are three of these tall bell towers. The towers are spiky, often with steeples, slightly Gothic in quality, a style rarely found on the mainland of Italy: there are only three important examples in Rome. Such towers, however, were built on churches in Sicily and Spain. In Malta the inspiration probably came from Italian text-books like Serlio, published in the sixteenth century, and Maltese architects first used towers on the old conventual church of St Lawrence in Il Borgo.[4] This building is now known to us only in prints, but it had tall western towers with steeples. St Lawrence was probably the prototype for the conventual church of St John in Valletta, which also has twin towers, and for the parish church of St George at Qormi built about the end of the sixteenth century. Qormi is one of the first of the big parish churches followed soon by Zebbug and Tarxien. The façade of Tarxien parish church is strange. The base appears to be too large for the superstructure of the towers, and at first glance one would assume that the towers are a later addition, but this is not so. At a later date a new façade was begun and carried to first-floor level, it being intended to wrap the new building around the old one.

The next group of parish churches to be built are among the most chaste, balanced compositions on the island and are the work of a very remarkable man: Tommaso Dingli. He was born in 1591 when a speedy fortification of the island was essential and, in common with other children who showed the slightest inclination towards architecture, he was, at an early age, sent to work in an artist's studio. Dingli showed remarkable promise, for at the age of 22 he designed the exquisite parish church of St Mary at Attard. The façade suggests a return to Renaissance purity and reminds one of the work of Alberti at Mantua some 150 years earlier. The fronts of both churches are similarly designed to suggest a Roman temple, a single rectangular statement topped by an all-embracing triangular pediment. Although at first sight this seems to be harking back to the Renaissance of Italy there had also been a revival there and Palladio had returned using this statement of the Roman temple front on some of his work in the Veneto. Dingli's parish church at Attard is beautifully modelled, the decorations of the doors

The dome and south transept of the
parish church at Zurrieq.

Crisp carving on the early seventeenth-century entablature of the old parish church at Birkirkara.

The south transept door at the parish church in Attard, right, and carving on the pedestal on the order of the main door.

and the architectural embellishments of the orders delicately and crisply executed. There is a hint of Spanish influence in all his work. A plateresque-like quality is evident on the façade of his next church, the old parish church which he designed at Birkirkara in 1617, where the doorway and its centre-piece have a pronounced Spanish flavour. Where this influence originated remains a mystery. Perhaps it was through friendship with some Spanish knights of the Order. It seems unlikely that at that early age he could have visited Spain.

Dingli's work was prolific. In addition to the two mentioned, he designed parish churches at Mosta and Naxxar. A short break occurs in his work which was taken up again in 1638 with the design of Gharghur parish church, shortly followed by Gudja and Zabbar. Dingli's main practice, at which he was most successful, was in designing and building this group of parish churches. His only job for the Knights of St John was the design of the old Porta S. Giorgio, now Kingsgate, the entrance to Valletta. Otherwise his work was entirely for his compatriots. Most of Dingli's churches have been considerably altered. As the villages grew, in some cases the churches proved too small for the congregation. At Birkirkara his church was abandoned, and a new one built. The old church is now a ruined shell, but most of the façade is still intact. Elsewhere aisles and more elaborate façades were added in the eighteenth or nineteenth century. At Zabbar, Dingli's dome was severely damaged by French cannons firing from the Cottonera Lines during the revolt of 1800, when Maltese insurgents besieged Valletta and the Three Cities, using Zabbar as their main base of operations. But in all cases, traces of Dingli's work can still be seen, usually in the transepts and the choir, and often in the lace-like patterning of the barrel vaults of the interiors. But Attard is the only one of his parish churches which remains complete and conveys an adequate impression of his capabilities. We have a contemporary portrait of Dingli showing a thin-faced man with high bones and hollow cheeks. The sensitivity of his mouth, half-hidden by a tidy beard and moustache, suggests an aesthetic. He has a worried look with furrowed brows and a high sloping forehead, his hair receding. Whether worry was endemic or merely characterized his feeling when the sketch was made we do not know, but he lived to the ripe old age of 75.

Throughout the seventeenth century more than a score of these large parish churches made their appearance in Malta. The parish church of St

Left: Dingli's original ceiling at Zabbar is still preserved in the nave.

Right: The interior of the fine modern dome at Zabbar.

Saviour at Lija is one of the best, retaining most of its original features. It was designed in 1694 by the Maltese architect Giovanni Barbara. One of his first important commissions carried out when he was in his 20's, it is a sober composition of simple design. Its tall character is accentuated by western towers which flank the façade and the dome is comparatively unassuming, rising well behind the cornice of the tall drum. Inside, the church is not ornate by Maltese standards. Unfluted Doric pilasters encircle the nave and transepts, and simple rings of mouldings lead the eye to the apex of the dome.

How different is this work from the more florid style that Barbara developed at St James in Valletta, and the seminary and Magisterial palace at Mdina.

The second half of the seventeenth century is dominated by the architecture of Lorenzo Gafà. His cathedrals at Mdina and Rabat in Gozo have already been described. In a series of large parish churches, Gafà showed his mastery of the Baroque: Siggiewi, San Nicola, St Lawrence at Vittoriosa and St Catherine at Zejtun. Most have been altered. The dome and façade at Siggiewi are much later, but Zejtun, his finest parish church, still retains its original qualities. Graceful and elegant, it depends for its effect upon good proportions, a product of the Roman Baroque with none of the efflorescence of Spanish work so abundantly displayed in the kingdom of the two Sicilies. Gafà has resisted the urge to over-carve the soft Maltese stone, and has retained a refreshing discipline in design. His crowning magnificence is the dome at Zejtun, a masterpiece of dynamic design, equalled only in Malta by his later dome on Mdina cathedral.

The climax of Maltese Baroque was reached by Dominico Cachia in his design for the new parish church of St Helen at Birkirkara, a larger and more commodious structure which replaced Dingli's earlier building at the other end of the town. St Helen's church lies at the end of a curving dark street which opens out to allow sun to flood the façade of the church, picking out its intricate flowing shapes and accentuating the stepping forward of the panels which build up the centrepiece. Cachia, it will be remembered, was later called to design, on the high point in Valletta, the splendid Baroque auberge of Castille and Leon. At Birkirkara the dome is powerful and well proportioned, but less dynamic than those designed by Lorenzo Gafà. The interior of the church is rich. Coupled Corinthian pilasters support the twin ribs of the vault panelled and incised with golden foliage. The vault and the

The simple dome of Lija church.

Left: The façade of the parish church of St Catherine at Zejtun, designed by Lorenzo Gafà and begun in 1692.

Right: The parish church of Our Saviour at Lija was built by Giovanni Barbara in 1694. Now that some of the surrounding buildings have been cleared it looks lost and lonely.

Left and right: The chancel and nave of Siggiewi church by Lorenzo Gafà.

The nave and choir at Zejtun.

The nave of the parish church of St Helen at Birkirkara.

Overleaf, page 202:
Domenico Cachia's dynamic Baroque front of the parish church of St Helen at Birkirkara lies at the end of a narrow street which opens out to form a small square in front of the church. Built between 1727 and 1745, it is the most impressive parish church in Malta.

Overleaf, page 203:
The Dominican monastery at Rabat.

apse are great fields of fresco, and the undersides of the arches leading to the aisles, and the domes and pendentives of these aisles, are copiously painted and carved. But the façade which is the crowning glory of this church for a man of 27 shows remarkable confidence.

Malta and Gozo are islands of churches and fortresses. The building of the churches was made possible only under the cloak of protection provided by the forts. There are probably more splendid examples of both to the square mile than almost anywhere in Europe. But to suggest that the Maltese scene consisted entirely of these structures would be to draw a misleading picture. There are numerous ancillary buildings, fine monasteries and convents, and in the countryside palaces and villas are numerous, in spite of the fact that members of the Order were precluded from living outside the town limits without special licence obtained only with difficulty. But the Maltese, growing prosperous, built for themselves and there are many beautiful villas with enclosed gardens well planted and irrigated, hidden from the public by high boundary walls. If Malta has, at first sight, an arid appearance, it is because the foliage is concealed behind the terraces and walls of stone.

Tradition is strong in Malta. Parish churches, crowned by monumental domes, are still built in the classical style and it is often difficult at first sight to establish the date for the various parts of churches. This stylistic continuity is admirable, as it gives a cohesion to the architecture of the islands. The parish churches still dominate the villages. The sudden change of scale from the small houses, which cluster around the bases of these large domed buildings, is exciting and stimulating, particularly so when suddenly one comes upon a church around the corner of one of the twisted streets which so characterize the villages. Consequently, it is sad to see that a fatal step has been taken in so many villages. Straight wide avenues have been driven through the existing mass of houses to create a monumental approach to the façade of a church. This is thought to enhance its importance, but it does the reverse. The monumental gash destroys the relationship between church and surrounding buildings, ruining the quality of the old villages which could be among the main tourist attractions of Malta. How pleasant the setting of a parish church faced by an informal square, a little planting, an occasional monument or cross, or perhaps a fountain and seats placed under the trees. Beyond twist the narrow lanes of the village opening out

The modern dome and drum of Gafà's church of St Nicholas at Siggiewi dominate the village.

from place to place to form the forecourt setting of a small, centrally planned Baroque church, or the punctuation point of a simple Maltese chapel. The smaller villages are jewels which should be handled with care and discrimination.

[1] Bonavia (C. G.) 'The Chapel of St Dominica at Zabbar "Unique Fresco Restored" ' in *Sunday Times of Malta* (7 July 1957).

[2] Buhagiar (Mario). 'Santa Marija Ta "Bir Miftuh" ' in *Sunday Times of Malta* (25 July 1965).

[3] Hughes (J. Quentin). 'The Church of St Catherine "Tat-Torba" and the origin of the Simplified Orders of Architecture' in *Arch*, Volume I (Malta 1954).

[4] Numerous early books on architecture were collected by the Knights and have since been deposited in the Valletta Library. These include the 1584 edition of the six books of architecture of Sebastiano Serlio which contain this illustration.

[5] Tonna (Joseph A.) 'Tommaso Dingli' in *Sunday Times of Malta* (5 September, 12 September and 19 September 1965).

Chapter 8: Calypso's Isle

Gozo, Malta's smaller sister, lies to the north, approximately half the size and always forced by the circumstances of history to play second fiddle to her more important neighbour. The two islands are separated by four miles of fast-running water in the Comino channels, across which plies the ferry between Marfa and Mgarr, the port of entry to Gozo. In the channels lie two smaller islands. Comino, the larger, less favoured even than Gozo, has a perpetual grudge against society. Its cluster of cottages is still referred to as 'the village', the nameless one unchristened by society. Even the new hotel on Comino stands well away from the village on the other end of the island, turning its back on the small group of inhabitants. But despite its harsh rocky outline and inhospitable character Comino was known in ancient times and Ptolemy calls it Cosyra. Perhaps because of its isolation it was used by the Grand Masters of the Order of St John as a game reserve.

Gozo has to the Maltese all the appearances of a foreign land. Its valleys are more lush and green, and in summer it retains its verdure when Malta becomes bleached by the sun. The soil is less easily washed away by heavy downfalls of rain and there is less need for terracing, which gives to the Maltese landscape its stony character. Throughout history it has been a land apart and even its people look quite different in appearance from their Maltese brethren. Short and stocky, the peasants, often without shoes, stand solidly upon the ground. Many of the women remind one of those classical female images portrayed by Picasso in his heroic period, but the girls are as beautiful as any for they are descendants from Calypso who seduced and held entranced the Greek mariner Odysseus. The nymph's cavern can still be seen high above the sandy bay of Ramla from which he must have gazed across the still blue sea longing for his homeland. Homer described it as 'a spot where even an immortal visitor must pause to gaze in wonder and delight'.[1]

However, there may be another reason for the strong dissimilarity between Gozitan and Maltese. Many times in her chequered history Gozo was raided by Muslim corsairs and her inhabitants carried off into captivity and it has been suggested that these raids were so destructive that the population had, on at least one occasion, to be replaced by immigration from Sicily.

In the fifteenth century her people suffered from such extreme poverty that they were unable to support themselves. Their crops devastated by Moorish invasions, the Gozitans had to plead for the remission of taxes due to the Viceroy of Sicily, and request the import of free grain.[2]

In 1551 a Turkish attack on Malta was foiled and the raiders turned their wrath on Gozo. The citadel was besieged and in desperation the Gozitans sued for peace. An Augustine monk, Friar Bartolomeo Bonavia, went out into the Turkish lines to agree terms, but the attackers broke their word, sacked the capital, burning all the documents, and carried the garrison and its people off into slavery. Milite Bernardo, the governor of the island, put his own wife and children to death rather than leave them to face captivity in the hands of the Turks, and went out to face the enemy in a last desperate, unequal, battle in which he fell. Some 5000 Gozitans were taken prisoner and the island was virtually depopulated, save for about forty old men who were left behind. Of the eighty-four churches on the island only forty-six remained standing and many of these were ruined. During the Great Siege of Malta in 1565 Gozo suffered little damage, as the Turk was fully occupied with his investment of the main island. After the siege was lifted, new fortification works were undertaken in Gozo and the citadel was strengthened. It is probable that Laparelli went there to advise on their design.

But Gozo traditionally feels that it is badly done by. This is England's Wales, Italy's Sicily, the less fortunate province, and yet it is this very isolation and its partial neglect by the Knights and the British, who had little need for an island without good harbours, that has left it in a more primitive state, less damaged by unsuitable development. Beautiful carved stone balconies, quite early in date, can still be found on some of the houses in

An early balcony on a house at Gharb in Gozo.

the Gozo villages. The tight, narrow, twisting streets of the old quarter of Victoria, often called Rabat, the capital, still retain a medieval quality, although most of the houses date from the seventeenth century and later. Victoria is one of the most charming towns in the archipelago. It stands on a prominence in the centre of the island, a natural citadel whose site has been further exploited by sheer walls of fortification which stand up against the skyline, a deterrent to any attacking force. The town was originally called Rabat and to its citadel fled the Gozo farmers and their families on the warning of Muslim invasion. Towers constructed along the coast line provided early warning of the approach of danger. Before the arrival of the Knights the countryside was undefended, Rabat in Gozo alone having meagre fortifications. A tax on wine had been imposed to build a fortified tower on Comino but work was never carried out and the money was spent by Alphonso V on other things.

In medieval times Gozo had lain for years in the hands of the Saracens, until Count Roger, the Norman, landed in 1090 and in a three-day campaign captured the island for Christianity, rebuilt the cathedral and dedicated it to the Blessed Virgin of the Assumption. Perched in the central citadel, the present building is a fine Baroque structure which dominates the skyline. It was rebuilt in 1711 from the designs of the Maltese architect Lorenzo Gafà, one of the great dome constructors of the Baroque, but, as one might expect in Gozo, the dome was never constructed and instead a flat ceiling painted in perspective closed the aperture. Although one misses the exciting silhouette that a dome would have provided, the false perspective is not without interest and ingenuity. It is obviously closely modelled on a drawing made by Pozzo, that Italian master of illusionism, in his treatise *Perspectiva pictorum*. Pozzo even includes a figure showing the setting out of the perspective, which must have considerably aided the artist working on the ceiling of Gozo cathedral.[5] The façade of the cathedral is impressive as it is always seen from below. A new cut has been made through the fortified wall of the citadel and the visitor suddenly finds himself in a small, irregularly shaped square, almost filled by a massive flight of steps which led to the west door of the church. The whole setting is beautifully sculptured and on each side stand older buildings, some still portraying the early roll or 'fat' mouldings of Maltese sixteenth-century architecture. The façade itself is very Italian; it stands as a screen to the church which

Victoria, the capital of Gozo, stands on a
prominence in the centre of the island, a
natural citadel whose site has been further
exploited by sheer walls of fortification.

From the citadel the screen façade of the
cathedral seems unrelated to the body of
the church. Gafà's dome was never built,
increasing this detachment.

Left: The public registry at Victoria. An early building displays characteristic Maltese 'fat' mouldings.

Right: Lorenzo Gafà's façade of the cathedral at Gozo, rebuilt in 1711.

St Cecilia tower at Ghajnsielem in Gozo.

lies beyond. It is a separate work of art, its proportions adjusted to its own magnificence and bearing little relation to the height of the nave roof which lies behind. This is also an Italian characteristic. The façade looks perfectly plausible from the front, but from an askewed view it stands up in a strange, isolated manner as though intended for a much larger building. Although the cathedral has no dome it does have a single bell tower towards its east end, which, because of its height, dominates the whole panorama of the citadel and reduces some of the impact of the absurdity of a high screen façade when seen from a distance.

With the coming of the Knights look-out towers were constructed around the coast, at least one of which had a double function: that of watching for the approach of the Turkish raiders and espying the Fungus Rock, a protected islet upon which grew the 'treasure of drugs' valued by the Knights for its prophylactic qualities. The shrub, known as *fungus melitensis*, was supposed to be a sovereign remedy against dysentery and haemorrhages of all kinds. The Order jealously protected it against intruders and the tower provided the guard for this purpose.

The cliffs of Gozo rise sheer for many hundreds of feet from the water's edge, unscalable and safe from assault. Only the little inlets like Xlendi, Mgarr, and Marsalforn needed protection. The Grand Master Alof de Wignacourt built for them small coastal forts in the early years of the seventeenth century. On each side of the Marsalforn fort stretch salt pans – shallow trays cut into the hard Gozo stone. They date from 1740, when the concession for the production of salt was granted. In the winter months the spray is blown high across the land, and settles in these pans. The summer sun evaporates it, leaving a deposit of salt. The shapes cut along the ridges of the stone cliff have a certain monumental grandeur. Like the foundations of some ancient city, they affect the geometrical properties of the redoubt which stands on the tip of the peninsula. Many of the Gozo villages lie along the spines of the hilltops. Quite different from those in Malta, Nadur, Xaghra, and Zebbug are amorphous shapes. The houses, following a street pattern, stretch out for a considerable distance and the villages appear to have no real core. Most of the buildings are comparatively modern, the inhabitants of Gozo having learned not to put their trust in permanent habitations where they became an easy prey to the heavy raids of the Muslims outside the citadel at Rabat. But bits of old Gozo still remain, such as

Overleaf, page 218:
A windmill at Qala in Gozo.

Overleaf, page 219:
Saltpans near the redoubt at Marsalforn.

the balconies of the old houses at Gharb and the circular windmill, its sail still intact, standing on the high ground above Qala.

Like Malta, Gozo has its fine parish churches. At Gharb the stumps of earlier towers form the bases for the Baroque fingers which reach up on each side of a flowery concave façade. This is the most exciting church tower on the island. The desire to build large churches has continued unabated in Gozo. Nadur parish church is a massive pile designed in the traditional Maltese Baroque. Although it was begun in 1760, most of the church dates from the late nineteenth century. Ta Pinù is a modern pilgrimage church standing in splendid isolation in open countryside not far from the village of Gharb. It is particularly impressive at sunset when golden light floods its neo-Romanesque exterior. Modelled on Lombardic work of the thirteenth century, it has the inevitable free-standing campanile; but it also includes transepts and over the crossing a squat octagonal crowns the dome. This

The cliffs of Gozo rise sheer for many hundreds of feet, unscalable and safe from assault. A rough sea at Dwejra point.

Fungus Rock.

The parish church at Gharb shows development through several styles.

de Palmeus's plan of the proposed fortified town at Chambray, drawn in 1754.

basilica of Ta Pinù replaced a primitive Gozo chapel, a single cell building modelled on the numerous fifteenth-century chapels which can still be found in Malta. In the year 1883 a peasant woman from Gharb heard a miraculous voice calling her to the church and from the end of the nineteenth century Ta Pinù has been a place of pilgrimage, a place to make thank-offerings for those saved from calamity, for sailors lifted from a perilous death in the foaming sea. The basilica, standing alone, is impressive by sheer size. Encasing the original chapel within its new structure it was begun in 1920, and was consecrated in 1931.

Gozo was the scene of the last town-planning project of the Knights. In 1722 there was an intense war scare and it looked as though the island would

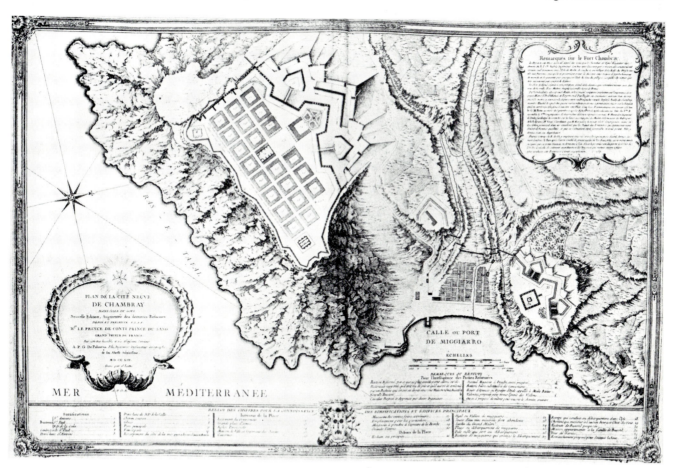

be attacked by Turkish forces in a series of retaliatory raids. The first consideration was towards improving the defences of Rabat and the citadel, but upon examination these were found to be expensive expedients unlikely to bear fruitful results, so instead it was decided to build a new fortified town on the promontory above the little harbour at Mgarr. There the water supply was good and, in the event of an attack, easy relief could be expected from nearby Malta. This was a fascinating project, the last new town to be commissioned by the Knights. In 1723 the French Knight de Tigné designed the new fortress at Mgarr, to be christened la Città Vilhena, after the Grand Master of the Knights. The town was to be laid out on a grid pattern of roads enclosing square plots of buildings built up to the street frontages. Except

The tombstones of British soldiers who died of fever at Fort Chambray.

for the addition of two further plots on the eastern end of the town adjoining a massive ammunition dump it was practically symmetrical. On an early drawing these two plots are omitted, probably because it was feared that they might be too near to the explosives. In the centre of the town a large square was intended, surrounded by porticoed buildings on three sides and the parish church on the fourth. Opposite the church was sited the palace of the governor, which extended into a cavalier placed above the main bastion of the landward defences. The elaborate trace of fortifications was deployed to the north, but on the other sides the ground rises so steeply that complex defensive works were unnecessary. In spite of the enthusiasm of the population and the ceremonial visit of the Grand Master Manoel de Vilhena the work was not put in hand. Probably Vilhena's exchequer was already too heavily committed with the building of a new fort in Marsamxett harbour and the extension of the land front of Valletta into the suburbs of Floriana. Not until September 1749 was money found by the Bali de Chambray out of his own purse and work went slowly ahead. Perhaps the man who pays the fiddler should call the tune. Anyway, the remnants of the new town, the plots now almost obliterated but the massive fortifications still intact, have since then been called Fort Chambray. The buildings which now stand house a mental hospital and among the weeds of an overgrown cemetery lie the bones of English soldiers, garrisons of the fort, their lives snuffed out at an early age by the devastating Malta fever. The craggy ramparts still stand as a reminder of this last stronghold of the Knights which, when the rest of Malta surrendered to the forces of Napoleon in 1798, continued to put up a stout resistance against the French attack.

1 Homer. *The Odyssey*, translated by E. V. Rieu (Harmondsworth, New York 1946), page 89.
2 Leopardi (E. R.) 'The Island of Gozo – 1432–1453' in *Melita Historica*, Volume 4, No.1 (1964), pages 67–71.
3 Gatt (J. E. H.) *Guide to Gozo* (Malta 1934), page 117.
4 Blouet (Brian). *Gozo* (Malta 1965). An excellent guide to the island.
5 Pozzo (Andrea). *Perspectiva pictorum et architectorum &c.* (Rome 1693).

Chapter 9: The British Influence

Events which followed the French Revolution caused the Knights of Malta to loose both influence and investments, for the French abolished the nobility and confiscated properties. Steeped in aristocratic precedent, it was natural that this Order should be the butt of French antagonism. Debts began to mount and the revenue of Malta was reduced to about one sixth of what it had been before the French Revolution. The fleet of the Knights consisted of two large ships, one still incomplete, two frigates, and a few galleys and their smaller sisters, galliots. Of the 600 Knights defending the island, two-thirds were French and of doubtful loyalty. In addition, there were 2210 regular troops supported by 10,000 militia, largely untrained. Neither in spirit nor in size was the force adequate to its task of defending the islands. The energetic Grand Master Emmanuel de Rohan tried hard to retrieve his fortunes. The English Langue was re-established and combined with that of Bavaria, and negotiations were opened with Russia in order to extend the influence of the Order. But the rise to power of Napoleon Bonaparte sealed the fate of the Order of St John in Malta. As country after country fell to his advancing army, the resources of the Knights diminished. Money to maintain and provision Malta and its garrison was hard to find. It is little wonder that there was internal intrigue and treachery. Discontent arose on the part of the French Knights, and mistrust was on all sides. This situation worsened with the death of de Rohan. The choice of successor was hardly propitious. A kind-hearted and sincere German, but lacking in determination and the sort of ruthless leadership that was needed to turn the events of history, Ferdinand von Hompesch became Grand Master in

1779. Surrounded by plotters who openly flouted their disloyalty, he did not know which way to turn. His lack of resolve exacerbated the slowing-down process. Little building work was done and it is perhaps ironic to notice that the last monument to be built by the Knights was the arch at Zabbar to the Grand Master Hompesch.

Meanwhile the great French expedition against Malta and Egypt was being fitted out in Toulon. 49,600 troops and 472 ships were assembled in fighting order and sailed from the home port. In late afternoon on 9 June 1798, this armada was sighted off Malta. The French fleet asked permission to enter the harbours. The Grand Master, half aware of the truth, vacillated, refused and then agreed to permit four vessels only at a time. With every intention of placing Hompesch in an impossible situation, the French issued an ultimatum. While this was going on, troops landed under cover of darkness at Ramla bay in Gozo, and at three bays of St Paul's, St Julian's, and Marsaxlokk in Malta. Practically unimpeded, they moved across the countryside and by dusk on the tenth it was all in their hands. The gates of Valletta and the Three Cities were closed and the garrison bottled up inside. Von Hompesch realized the futility of resistance, the blood that would be spilt to no avail, and next morning he agreed to an armistice. Capitulation was inevitable. With hardly a shot fired, the greatest concentration of defensive works in Europe fell. Within three days the Knights were bundled out and sailed from Malta. The French took from its forts 1200 guns, 40,000 muskets and 1,500,000 tons of powder.

On 13 June, Napoleon entered the city of the Knights, the stronghold which epitomized the ancient regime with all its aristocratic privileges. All signs of the past were speedily removed. Escutcheons were defaced, inscriptions cut from the stone, the privileges of the Church absolved, the Pope's jurisdiction withdrawn, revolutionary laws enacted, and the streets renamed. The French troops were making themselves unpopular. They were arrogant and abused their power, and their zeal for reformation came too rapidly for a people steeped in history and tradition. The Maltese dislike of the Knights was soon outweighed by their loathing of the French. It was humiliating to see their church vestments sold by auction and their precious plate removed as loot. A quarter of a million pounds' worth of goods were packed aboard the French warship *Orient*, which sailed with the fleet to Egypt. Then Nelson struck. At the Battle of the Nile the French fleet was decimated and Britain gained naval control of the Mediterranean. In the battle *Orient* was sunk, taking with her the rich treasure of Malta.

Meanwhile fighting had broken out in Malta. The insurgents began to organize themselves and soon the countryside was in their hands. The French were enchained in Valletta and the Three Cities, and the siege began. This act in itself did not greatly dismay the French commander, General Vaubois, for this was soon to become a war of attrition, and with fewer mouths to feed his chance of survival increased. Stage by stage he expelled undesirable Maltese, the young, the old, and the infirm from the citadel his troops held around the harbours.

Vaubois' main problem was supplies, for without them he could not survive. There seemed little chance of a direct frontal attack by the Maltese.

His well-trained troops could withstand this. A novel form of warfare was being developed by the British. The Continental Blockade instituted in retaliation to Napoleon's Berlin Decree of 1806, which set out to isolate Britain from Europe, was the beginning of a stranglehold asserted by the British fleet against the forces of Napoleon.

A delegation from the Maltese insurgents sailed for Italy, seeking help from King Ferdinand of Naples. En route they fell in with the British battle-fleet off Sicily, and Nelson was hailed. He agreed to help them. From the quarterdeck of HMS *Vanguard* off Stromboli island, on 16 September 1798, he wrote: 'I have entreated the Portuguese to go off to Malta, which with little exertion must be taken from the French, but I hope your Lordship will not build hope on their exertions. The moment I can get ships, all aid shall be given to the Maltese. What would I give for four bomb-ships! All the French armament would long ago have been destroyed'[1].

Ships of the Portuguese allies in whom Nelson had little confidence appeared off the coast of Malta and landed guns. On 24 October Nelson sent in Captain Alexander Ball aboard HMS *Alexander*, supported by a frigate, a sloop, and a fire-ship. The situation was precarious. The French had 3000 infantry and five companies of gunners, while the Maltese were attacking with 3200 men nominally under arms, though most of them were poorly equipped. A plot to seize Valletta was frustrated, and forty-five Maltese were arrested and shot in the Palace square. Naples itself lay in the path of the advancing French army and soon fell. Everything was in an uproar as the Court of Ferdinand hurriedly moved to safety at Palermo. The note of confidence seen in Nelson's letters gradually ebbed. In September he was writing: 'I am now pressing Malta very hard and it shall soon surrender. I approve very much of your directing guns to be landed from the *Alexander*. I would have every exertion used and every nerve strained to finish this tedious blockade.'

With the Rear Admiral the Marquis de Niza threatening to withdraw his ships from the blockade the Portuguese participation was in doubt. In October of the following year Nelson wrote to Niza:

'As the reduction of the Island of Malta is of the greatest consequence to the interests of the Allied Powers at War with France, and the withdrawing of the Squadron of his Most Faithful Majesty under your command, at this time, from the blockade of that Island, will be of the most ruinous con-

A British man-o-war at the time of Nelson.

sequences to their interests, particularly when an Enemy's fleet of thirteen Sail of the Line are duly expected in those seas, and two Sail of the Line and several other Ships with provisions and stores, for the relief of Malta are now loading at Toulon; you are hereby requested and directed, in consideration of the above circumstances, and not withstanding the orders you may have received from your Court to return to Lisbon, not on any consideration whatever to withdraw one man from that Island.'

By 26 October 1799 Nelson was desperate.

'We shall lose it, I am afraid, past redemption ... If Ball can hardly keep the inhabitants in hope of relief by the five hundred men landed from our Ships what must be expected when four hundred of them, and four Sail of the Line will be withdrawn? And if the Islanders are forced again to join the French we may not find even a landing a very easy task, much less to get again our present advantageous position ... This is the only thing in my opinion for consideration. If we lose this opportunity it will be impossible to recall it'. Requesting aid he wrote to the Emperor of Russia. Troops were promised but never arrived. But gradually the British blockade began to have its effect. Off Cap Pessaro, only four miles from the coast of Sicily, the French ship *Genereux* was captured. She was bearing the flag of Rear-Admiral Perrée and carrying 2000 troops with provisions and stores for the relief of hard-pressed Valletta. French ships trying to slip out of Valletta were attacked and captured, and on land the build up of forces began.

Cruising off Malta, Nelson wrote:

'The *Emerald* will sail in twenty-four hours after my arrival for Malta. At least two thousand of small arms complete, ammunition etc., should be sent by her. This is wanted to defend themselves: for offence two or three large mortars, fifteen hundred shells, with all necessaries, and perhaps a few artillery, two 10-inch howitzers with a thousand shells. The Bormola and all the left side of the Harbour with this assistance will fall. Ten thousand men are required to defend these works, the French can only spare twelve hundred; therefore a vigorous assault in many parts, some one must succeed.'

In December two British regiments arrived from Minorca and assembled at Zabbar, Zejtun and Gudja, holding the southern line from the coast to Hamrun. The Maltese troops were dug in on the northern line to the coast at St Julian's bay. The investment was complete and the grip tightened. The prospect of relief from France dwindled, and on 4 September 1800 General Vaubois capitulated. There had been bombardment and counter-bombardment. The dome of Tomasso Dingli's parish church at Zabbar had been ruptured and largely destroyed. Many buildings had been ruined, but there had been no general assault upon the fortifications of Valletta and the Three Cities. Once more this giant ring of defences had succumbed, not to a frontal attack, but through attrition.

An uneasy peace between Britain and France followed, and negotiations were set in motion to decide the fate of Malta. In the islands themselves strong feeling had grown up in favour of remaining under British rule. The French were not averse to the Knights returning so long as the fortifications were demolished. Others favoured control by Naples. As the arguments continued, Great Britain began to see more clearly the advantage of holding on to this strategic fortress whose position in the Middle Sea gave control of movement throughout the Mediterranean. Napoleon was fully aware that Malta was the node of any southern European policy.

'I would rather see', he said, 'the British on the heights of Montmartre than in Malta.'

The Treaty of Amiens ruled that Malta should be returned to the Knights but the British stood their ground in Valletta. Possession was nine-tenths of the law. Evacuation of Malta or war was the issue, and then once more the French and British were at each other's throats.

The final eclipse of Bonaparte's power came with his defeat at Waterloo. British sovereignty over the islands of Malta and Gozo was confirmed by the Treaty of Paris and, amid a wave of popularity, Sir Alexander Ball was made first Civil Commissioner.[2]

There are long if somewhat tenuous links between Britain and both the Knights of St John and the island of Malta. From the time of the First Crusade, Englishmen fought in the battles of the Holy Land and enlisted under the banner of the Order, carrying on their coat of arms the escutcheon of the Kings of England. Early in the twelfth century English Knights established a priory or hospital at Clerkenwell, just outside the City of London, and built there a round temple church which was consecrated in 1185. The crypt of this Norman church still survives. But from 1536 the first serious rupture became apparent, with the dissolution of the English monasteries and the severance of links with Rome. In 1540 the blow fell on the Order of St John and an act of dissolution throughout England, Wales, and Ireland received the Royal assent. Some Knights fled the country and joined their brothers in Malta, but by then the English Langue was already shrunken. From a contingent of 119 members living in England in 1338 the Order had been reduced to thirty-four Knights and fourteen preceptors by the beginning of the sixteenth century, and in the year of dissolution by King Henry VIII there were a mere twenty-six members here, including Priors, Commanders and Knights.[3] Thus there were few Englishmen in Malta at the time of the Great Siege of 1565. Of the two Knights present, the Bailiff of Eagle was killed in action and Sir Oliver Starkey stood beside the Grand Master la Valette as his secretary, a pillar of strength and a valuable confidant. Sir Robert Schelley, the Prior of England, had been cooped up in Naples unable to help the besieged garrison of Malta.[4]

Throughout the Knights' tenure of the island British ships and men-of-war paid periodic visits to the Grand Harbour, and were often received with kindness and hospitality, but the link had grown stronger with British naval supremacy in the Mediterranean and now the task fell to England to govern, maintain, garrison, and defend this stronghold in the Middle Sea.

The British military authorities were both embarrassed and overawed by the extent of the Malta fortifications. Miles upon miles of ramparts and strong-points seemed to call for a prodigious garrison to safeguard them against attack. This attitude of mind was understandable, for Britain had grown to power through the strength of her navy and her ability to land striking forces in Europe. The whole of Britain was a citadel so that there was little need for high competence on the part of military engineers to build fortifications comparable to those still being carried out in Continental Europe. These countries, vulnerable to attack from the land, still encircled their frontier towns with rings of fortifications and protected their river crossings and vulnerable valleys with forts and outposts. Frenchmen in particular excelled in the art of fortification, an art largely lost to the British army whose task after the Napoleonic campaign lay mainly in the subjection of unruly and ill-equipped savages. The situation drew various wild statements from military leaders who should have known better. On the one hand there were those who found the complex of fortifications inherited from the Knights too large to cope with and too cumbersome to garrison against any serious threat. On the other hand, some claimed them quite out-dated and incapable of valuable use in modern warface. The first balanced assessment of the situation did not appear until 1859 when a report on the state of the Fortress of Malta was issued by the War Office.[5] The writer castigated ill-founded criticism. 'To talk of the fortifications in scorn or derision', he wrote, 'or to look upon them as a labyrinth of confusion, arising out of the crochets of successive Grand Masters, is not worthy of soldiers who understand their profession.' Although not perfect by modern standards, the fortifications had undoubted merits. 'Improvements in small arms and artillery, and the progress of military science in general would perhaps dictate to an able engineer a different trace from that which exists, bastions would be made fewer and of greater size, and detached works would be substituted for continuous lines of advanced works'–

'Now a general impression has grown up that Malta is a weak place and that England exacts an impossible task from her army in allocating a garrison of five or six thousand men to the defence of what, all over Europe, is considered nearly an impregnable fortress. The idea of defending twenty-five miles of parapet is considered to settle the question at once as absurd, and still no assertion is more fallacious. Manning the parapets throughout their length is not the way of defending them. The science of fortification has as its object to enable small numbers to oppose large, and, by placing a few men in an advantageous sheltered position, to enable them to oppose large masses of troops. In all well-constructed bastioned fronts the whole extent of the front, measuring perhaps along the parapet five hundred yards, can be seen and commanded by two short flanks, about one tenth of that length, and when one line of works envelops another it is not necessary, even in a general assault, to man the interior line until the exterior is carried.

'The first and most important measure we recommend is the formation of a clear and complete project of defence under every possible form which the attack may take. It is quite possible that the real attack might take the form not foreseen, but, as in a game of chess, the player who knows how to reply to the known openings of the game will, in general, be the one who is most prepared for any description of attack, so that in the great game of war the surest mode of being prepared for an unforeseen attack is to consider thoroughly those attacks which may be foreseen.'[6]

Two forms of attack could be expected. From the sea when the main defence would be from coast guns well served and adequately supplied with ammunition. Wherever possible, guns should be hidden until it was necessary to bring them into action. Although it would mean a gigantic undertaking, the other danger was an attack from the land.

The report then outlines a full plan of defence against such an eventuality dealing with police precautions, censoring of mail, retention of aliens, surveillance of suspected persons, conservation of valuable water supplies, the clearance of ground in the line of fire of the guns, and assurance to the civilian population about their own safety and about compensation for damage to private property. Strong detachments would be sent out to reconnoitre and if possible harass the enemy advance, and a company of the best marksmen should be formed to pick off any enemy staff engineer or officer who might approach the defences. The garrison, some 6000 men, should be disposed irrespective of barrack accommodation with 2000 in Valletta, 2000 on the Cottonera Lines and, in their rear, 1000 at Floriana and smaller garrisons at the forts of Ricasoli, Manoel, and Tigné. In the mass of instructions an interesting note of warning appears: 'Writers of experience think it necessary to caution officers against the misappropriation of valuable bomb-proofs which arise at such times from selfish or private feelings.

Bomb-proof cover is required, first for gunpowder, second for the sick, third for provisions, fourth for the combatants, and fifth for warlike stores subject to damage.'

An attack across open country on to the land front of Floriana was considered a Herculean task, but the most judicious measure an enemy could take in order to capture its main objective, Valletta. 'It must be the work of months – it might be a work of years, but no obstacle has yet been opposed by the hand of man which cannot, by patience and skill, be overcome. Supposing the ditch to be 120 feet deep and 60 feet wide, 2400 cubic yards of material would span it by an embankment 60 feet wide at the top and 300 at the bottom. An intelligent enemy would lay his plans long before; possibly they may be already made! He would foresee that this work could be carried on night and day, without the slightest danger from sorties to which the ditch itself is an insuperable barrier, in a very great degree by machinery. He would perhaps come prepared with tramways and tip carts. He would blind and cover his tramway. Railway apparatus under fire would be a novelty, perhaps, but what we are speaking of is perfectly practicable. It is a mere question of time and engineering plant. It would perhaps be the work of a week in ordinary railway work, and, working night and day for a month, the embankment could easily be made, even during a siege. While recommending that the experience of the past be strictly followed in the defence of the works of Valletta, we think it right to call attention to new powers which science has put at the disposal of the engineer. We therefore think that the Valletta ditch, though perhaps one of the most formidable artificial obstacles in the world, is not an insuperable one. It is for this reason that we entreat that no opportunity be lost of defending work by work, inch by inch, every covert, way and counterguard.'

Short of actual invasion by a powerful enemy force, the main danger was a coup de main – a surprise attack when the gates of the cities would be rushed and the small garrisons overcome.[7] Thus in the mid-nineteenth century the main task lay in strengthening the gateways and their adjoining guard posts. This is why many of the Valletta gates were re-built during the reign of Victoria. 'At the gate a keep should be constructed capable of lodging a company of the garrison at least, and so constructed that they would be placed over the gateway in an unassailable position, for whence they would secure the command and bar the entrance into the town.'[8]

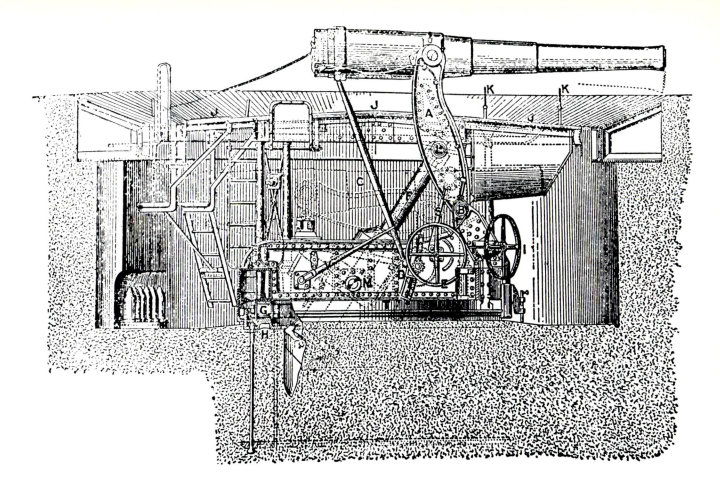

A 6-inch breech-loading gun.

In the first half of the century the minimum garrison was considered to be 6000 troops, although in 1853 there were only 3000 British soldiers on the island, sufficient to hold Valletta and Floriana and leaving none to spare for the defence of the other side of the Grand Harbour and Fort Manoel. Thirteen years later a force of 12000 was being called for to safeguard Malta and the main depot of the Mediterranean fleet if the British ships should be in action elsewhere. Militia laws were passed to recruit Maltese infantry and artillery men and in 1873 the Governor, Van Straubenzee, reported that 'there is no difficulty in recruiting the men, who are fine able-bodied, steady soldiers, from whom good service may be expected. The Maltese gave good proof of their soldierly qualities in their operations against the French which, combined with the blockade by the British fleet, brought about the surrender of the island.'[9]

Malta was needed as a British stronghold. Her Grand Harbour afforded safe anchorage for the largest of fleets. Her gunpowder stores in the Cottonera Lines safeguarded the whole munitions of the fleet. The magazine of the Grand Polverista was, for example, capable of holding some 21,000 barrels of powder. The island had become a valuable staging point for both the Army and the Navy, and was used for the assembly of the allied fleet and the preparation of Empire troops prior to the assault on the Crimea in 1854. Her fine climate made her an admirable centre where, in good hospitals, the sick could be nursed back to health. With the opening of the Suez Canal in 1869 Malta's importance to Britain increased. Taking advantage of the shortest sea route, soldiers and munitions could be speeded to the ends of the earth to implement British imperial policy and safeguard her possessions. Ships could call for coal and replenish their stores on the long journey to the East, and Malta eased the demands on Britain which grew as the result of a series of minor wars in the second half of Victoria's reign – in China and New Zealand, the expedition to Abyssinia in 1867, the Zulu War in 1879, British occupation of Egypt in 1881, the Sudanese War of 1884 and the South African Wars of 1880 and 1899. To serve the fleet new docks were constructed and the Royal Naval Dock was completed and opened in 1871.

Throughout this period capabilities, both in attack and defence, rapidly developed. Large new cannons had to be forged in England and shipped out to Malta where new platforms and expensive magazines had to be constructed. At the outbreak of the Crimean War Lord Raglan, the Commander in Chief, and his Director General of Artillery called at Malta and passed adverse comment on the strength of the powder magazines, which were pretty much in the same state in which they had been found in 1798 when captured from the French. Bomb-proof covers were needed to protect them from enemy bombardment. The cost of strengthening Malta was high and the military authorities used their ingenuity to make what economies they could. It was pointed out that two new ditches, which were required for the defence of Valletta from Marsamxett harbour, would 'serve the inhabitants for bathing places' and consequently the military considered it reasonable that the civil authorities should foot half the bill.[10] By mid-century,

332 pieces of artillery were defending Malta, including six of the heavy Lancaster guns. But this left her with only a third more guns than Gibraltar in spite of her large number of forts and fortified lines.[11] By 1860 work was going ahead on the task of re-stocking Malta with new and more powerful guns and strengthening the gun positions to take them. Because of the great weight of these new guns some new batteries had to be re-built from virgin rock.[12]

The tempo quickened, the science of war strode forward in ever-increasing paces. Techniques changed and no sooner were guns installed than they were out-dated. After 1866 iron boats began to replace timber ones and bigger coast guns were needed both to penetrate their protective iron plates and subdue the larger armament they carried. As the range of ships guns increased, the coast guns had to be placed farther from the harbour which it was their task to protect. Rifle barrels began to replace smooth-bored guns.[13] Breech-loading guns with their advantage of more rapid fire began to replace muzzle loaders, but it was not until after 1881 that the changeover took place on the big guns.

To illustrate the problem which arose during the restocking of the Malta artillery it is necessary to describe naval developments. Before 1866 five inches of iron plate had afforded adequate protection, but in that year, with the introduction of twenty-three ton guns, twelve inches of iron were needed for protection. Twelve years later it was known that the Italians were about to commission warships mounting 100-ton guns against which a protection of twenty-eight inches of iron was needed. To make matters worse, these ships of the 'Duillio' class were themselves protected by twenty-two inches of steel – formidable assailants. It was also realized that steam-powered ships were capable of putting in simultaneous attacks on several parts of the island and landing troops at various points. The British defence policy had therefore to be drastically modified. In January 1868 the military authorities had recommended the establishment of four strong forts encircling Valletta and the Three Cities, placed on high ground mainly between the villages and stretching from Zabbar in a wide half-circle to the heights above Sliema. However, it soon became clear that these forts were too close to the Grand Harbour to give adequate protection. In 1873 the advantages of fortifying the ridge of commanding ground which runs across the island north of Mdina and some four to seven miles from Valletta were being seriously considered. 'A few detached forts on this line would cut off all that westerly portion of the island where there are good bays and facilities for landing. This line of forts would retain the resources of the greater part of the country and the water on the side of the defenders, and the ground would be much cheaper than that in the immediate neighbourhood of Valletta.' This line of fortifications, later to be known as the Victoria Line, had previously been considered by the Knights of St John and a portion in the area around Naxxar had already been fortified. Forts and strong points on the Victoria Line were now constructed – Mosta, Bingemma and Magdalena. Large new guns were hurriedly imported from the arsenals of England. Eight-thirty eight-tonners with a calibre of twelve inches, and eleven

The long low outline of Fort Leonardo.

A 38-ton muzzle-loading gun at Fort
Delimara.

twenty-five-tonners measuring eleven inches were brought in and soon
positioned in barbettes or behind shields. New high-placed coastal forts
rose to the south of the Grand Harbour to supplement these long-range
defences, Fort Leonardo housing three twenty-five-tonners and Fort Rocco
with three of the mighty thirty-eight-ton guns. The defence works had now
been pushed so far forward that one military adviser suggested that the
fortifications of Valletta and Floriana might at least in part be pulled down
to make way for housing.[14] This advice was fortunately never accepted,
preserving for our day almost intact the magnificent military architecture
of Laparelli and Floriani.

The island of Malta, which in 1814 had been accepted with some reluctance by Britain for the protection of the Maltese people, had now become
the pivot of imperial defence. The position was clearly stated in a memorandum of 1878.[15] 'The difficulty of maintaining a fleet in the Mediterranean,
without the possession of Malta, would, in the present day, be almost
insurmountable, and if in other hands, it would, from its position, be a most

The dreadnought HMS *Monarch* in the Grand Harbour before seeing action with the Grand Fleet at Jutland.

dangerous point from which the commercial route to Suez and the Levant might be obstructed.' The build-up of the fleet continued. By 1879 there were four large warships and a garrison of 6500 men. Ten years later Malta held 10,777 men, strongest of all garrisons in the English colonies.[16] By 1904 it was nearly 17,000 with ten large warships forming the Mediterranean fleet, and by 1929, its point of maximum build-up, eighty-six naval vessels including ten large ones lay at anchor in the waters of the Grand Harbour and Marsamxett, their safety secured by a garrison of 21,045 soldiers.[17]

Architecturally, the Victorian forts make little impact. Of low silhouette, they are sited for concealment rather than monumental effect. Unlike their medieval predecessors, their deterrance lay hidden, ready to rise when needed from barbettes or concealed iron shields. In medieval defence, victory often lay in the awesome presence of the fort itself – in modern war the deterrent is known but not shown.

The monuments the British left are more in evidence – early essays are in the neo-Classical style like the little Greek temple whose dignified silhouette shades the statue to the first Governor, Sir Alexander Ball. This stands in peaceful greenery on the Lower Barracca, looking out across the mouth of the Grand Harbour and close by the fortified curtain built and named by Ball. The warm stone of Malta suits this style of architecture and the Greek columns, now weathered by the lashing sea-laden wind, are absorbed as an integral part of Valletta's scene. The effigy of the Marquis of Hastings rises as though woken from a bad dream to gaze between the classic pillars of his enshrouding monument. This too is Neo-Grec., its artist and date unknown but clearly early nineteenth century and probably erected soon after the death of the Marquis in 1826.

The main guard stands in the palace square, a stately Doric portico attached to an older building of the Knights, the former chancellery. The

A little Greek temple on the Lower Barracca in Valletta shades the statue of the first Governor, Sir Alexander Ball.

guard is crowned by the royal coat of arms cut in the soft Malta stone and below an inscription dated 1814 records in Latin the compact between Malta and Great Britain.

When the British arrived they found an adequate supply of fine public buildings, so no great building programme had to be undertaken. The one exception was the need for an Anglican church, as the Maltese were Roman Catholic to a man. Garrison chapels provided for the needs of the army and navy, but it was felt that something more splendid should grace the capital of this proud colony. Consequently Richard Lankersheer, a dilettante with considerable architectural taste though little or no practical knowledge, was called in with the request to design an Anglican cathedral above the shores of Marsamxett. Work began on Lankersheer's design, but soon cracks appeared in the stone work and two naval architects, hurriedly called for consultation, condemned the building as unsafe. Understandably there was a considerable furore, Lankersheer was taken ill and died. It was rumoured that he had committed suicide. The year was 1841. William Scamp was one

245

William Scamp's chancel façade of the Anglican cathedral in Valletta.

of the Admiralty architects who had surveyed the building and he now took the reins and produced a new design. Most of what had been already built had to be cleared and work started once more from fresh foundations. To add to the complications the Bishop of Gibraltar sent instructions that the church was to be switched round so that the main portico of Ionic columns which faces the auberge d'Aragon is no more than a false screen hiding the apse of Scamp's cathedral whose main entrance is now round the back. In 1842 Queen Adelaide visited Valletta and laid the foundation stone of the new building. William Scamp was a fine architect. The previous year he had built the naval steam bakery whose walls lap the waters of Dockyard creek; surely the most splendid bakery in existence! Scamp's work on the cathedral reflects that of his contemporaries in London; men like Hardwick and Inwood whose capabilities in the Greek style must surely have influenced this visitor to Malta. The portico is impressive and so also is the plain monumental interior of the nave, uncluttered by galleries which do so much to disfigure contemporary churches in England.[18] The tall tower with its pointed stone spire might seem at first sight to have been an English semi-Gothic importation, and certainly there are overtones of churches like St Mary-le-Bow. But the tower and spire of the Anglican cathedral are really typically Maltese, part of a long tradition which started with the conventual church in Vittoriosa, appeared on St John's, Valletta, until the spires had to be removed after the last war's bombardment, and is found in a number of the country parishes. The spire certainly has a dramatic effect on the Valletta skyline, its tall, pointed shape in sharp contrast to the pile-up of rectangular masses in the flat roofs of the surrounding houses.

The Classical style was ideal for use on large porticoes which gave welcome shade to most of the military buildings erected under British rule. The Pembroke barracks of 1860 and the barracks and hospital at Imtarfa built thirty-three years later follow a pattern established by anonymous Royal Engineer designers. The buildings are admirable, well proportioned, spacious and dignified, a happy marriage of Victorian and vernacular architecture. No one has yet studied this period in great detail, and it is not clear what hand Maltese architects had in the work. However, we know that the conversion of the Villa Bighi into a naval hospital was the work of a Maltese architect, Gaetano Xerri. The villa, a fine eighteenth-century building lying at the head of Kalkara creek, was tastefully converted by the addition of a neo-Classical portico to its main façade and verandahed blocks on each side. However, its dignity is now marred by a large, brightly painted, iron shed in the forecourt.

The Gothic Revival, that most English of English styles, stands out like a sore thumb in Malta. Various churches and a cemetery were constructed under British influence in the second half of the century. Occasionally the spiky, filigree quality of their Gothic decoration acts as a pleasing foil to the massive monumentality of the Maltese blocks, but generally the results are unsympathetic. One wonders what could have prompted the erection of that little Gothic house pinched in to a street frontage in the fine Baroque square in front of the cathedral at Mdina. It would hardly have been more incongruous to have found an English vicarage on the doorstep of St Peter's.

The 1880's were vintage years for English culture in Malta, based on the imported amenities of late Victorian civilization. As one might expect the emphasis was on sanitation and hygiene, communications, and housing. The demand for water grew and in 1881 the distillation of sea water began. In the following year electric street lighting was introduced, and a year later saw the building of the railway line from Valletta to Mdina, a short-lived venture abandoned in the inter-war years. The Italians made great play of their claim to have successfully bombed the track and station in 1941, in spite of the fact it had not been used for many years. Suburban sprawl, so characteristic of England, spread across the hinterland of the capital. Terrace houses lined the roads that were built to serve the rapidly increasing population. The one attempt at establishing a model working-class layout, Albert Town, begun in 1875 was a failure and, although a few streets were laid out and some housing begun, work was soon abandoned.

Mosta church and the opera house in Valletta are the two most important buildings of the period. Both were gross, very large, and rather coarse in detail. Mosta is a vast globular design, modelled on the Roman Pantheon and every bit as large. It was designed by Grougnet de Vassé and the foundation stone was laid in 1833.[19] It was a stupendous undertaking and was carried out almost entirely by voluntary labour. The complexity of the task increased through the necessity of building the new church over an older one, which in the meantime had to be retained and used for church services. This is often the case in Malta and Gozo, creating a strange situation of one church engulfing another, a kind of giant spider's web spun year by year until on completion the old encased church is devoured. The thick drum of the Mosta church was made sufficiently wide for lorries to be able to travel its circumference carrying on them the stone needed for its construction. The dome, itself some 118 feet in diameter, was designed to be built without scaffolding or centring and consists of a succession of overlapping courses slowly closed to meet at the apex. The interior is immensely impressive for its sheer size, but on the exterior the architect has repeated the fault previously perpetrated on the Pantheon – the addition of a columnal portico which seems to be no part of the great drum. To make matters worse Groupnet de Vassé, influenced by the style of his day, used a large measure

The spire of the Anglican cathedral has a dramatic effect on the Valletta skyline, its pointed shape in sharp contrast to the pile-up of rectangular masses in the flat roofs of the surrounding houses.

of Greek design, and the portico of Greek proportions lies uncomfortably between clumsy squat towers. The acroteria which decorate the pediment are lumpy and coarsely carved and the acanthus frieze around the dome is vulgar and grotesque.

The Valletta opera house was equally impressive. During the last war it was severely damaged and has since been pulled down. An earlier writer summed up its character most aptly – 'Coming suddenly upon this building for the first time, one experiences a shock of surprise. It is so obviously British that one might well be in London, or Manchester, or Liverpool, were it not for the whiteness of the stone, which alone tends to dispel the illusion.'[20] The child of Edward Middleton Barry, architect of the Royal Opera House, Covent Garden, the Valletta building was commenced in 1860 at a projected cost of about £60,000. Barry's first solution demonstrated the danger of preparing a design in an office some thousands of miles from the site. He had no experience of Malta, no sympathy for the vernacular, and was blissfully unaware of the fact that the streets of Valletta are steep sloping. His opera house was designed for a flat site. When told the difficulties his expedient was to raise the building on a high stepped podium creating an even greater sense of isolation from its surroundings. The building was opened in October 1866 with the splendid glittering performance of Bellini's *I Puritani*, but seven years later it was gutted by a disastrous fire. However, the rebuilding followed the original design and Valletta had for many years a fine, spacious auditorium on the classical model with five tiers of boxes encircling the seating in the stalls.

Malta must have been a gay, intriguing place attracting to her shores all types of Englishmen. The glamour of its past evinced in the magnificence of its architectural heritage, the warmth of its sun, the steadfastness of its British protection, and the social life of its garrison attracted most of the English poets and writers at one time or another. Coleridge was in the vanguard a mere three years after the capture of the island from the French. On landing he wrote 'One's first feeling is, that this is all strange; and when you begin to understand a little of the meaning and the uses of the massy endless walls and defiles, then you feel and perceive that this is very wonderful. A city all of freestone, all the houses looking new; all with flat roofs, the streets all straight, and at right-angles to each other; but many of them exceedingly steep, none quite level; of the steep streets, some are stepped with the smooth, artificial stone, some having the footpath on each side in stone steps, the middle left for carriages; lines of fortifications, fosses, bastions, curtains, etc. etc., endless; – . . . the whole island looks like one monstrous fortification . . . the fortifications of Valletta are endless . . . such vast masses, bulky mountain breasted heights.'[21] Coleridge was intrigued by what he saw and perhaps induced others to follow. Lord Byron was there in 1809 and again two years later, struggling with his deformed foot up the sun-drenched streets of Valletta to write with despair 'Adieu, ye cursed streets of stairs (how surely he who mounts you swears). Adieu.' Lady Hester Stanhope, that eccentric and remarkable Englishwoman, called at Malta in 1810 en route for the Middle East.

Left and right: Valletta 'the streets all straight, and at right angles to each other; but many of them exceedingly steep, none quite level . . .' – Coleridge

Twenty years later the second generation of visitors began to appear. Disraeli in 1830 describes his visit to the Union Club in the old auberge de Provence in Valletta. 'This is, in every sense of the word, not an inferior establishment, even the building (which is an old palace), to the London Union.' Already we see the exclusiveness of the English occupation. The establishment of English institutions and the divorce from social participation in the life of the colony. In a memorandum written on 22 February 1878, Sir Lintorn Simmons, then Inspector General of Fortifications and later to be Governor of the island, wrote, with reference to the danger of attack from Italy. 'There is one point, however, in connection with this subject which cannot fail to attract the attention of visitors to the island, and that is the almost absolute estrangement in society of the purely British and native elements. This is very much to be regretted, but is exceedingly marked. Maltese officers and gentlemen are not admitted to the English clubs, and the result is that strong anti-British feelings may be engendered in secret, almost unknown to the British community.' The report was read by the King, who instructed that it should be sent to the Secretary of State but, no doubt, this short paragraph attracted little attention and received no redress. Certainly the exclusiveness of the English tended to remain up to the conclusion of the second world war, to the detriment of both Malta and England. Besides visiting the Union Club, Disraeli was impressed by Valletta, which, he wrote 'equals in its noble architecture, if it does not excel, any capital in Europe . . . For if Valletta, with its streets of palaces, its picturesque forts and magnificent churches, only crowned some green and azure island of the Ionian Sea, Corfu for instance, I really think that the ideal of landscape would be realised.'

Sir Walter Scott came in the next year and described this 'splendid town quite like a dream'. In Malta he collected material for a novel on the siege by the Turks, a story which he never completed. In 1844 Thackeray was there, and four years later Edward Lear made the first of his numerous visits to the island recording his impressions in a series of exquisite water-colours, many of which are now displayed in the Valletta Museum. The crowning visit was in April 1903 when King Edward VII became the first English reigning monarch to visit Valletta. Our most powerful fleet was based there, dressed out in brilliant array to greet his visit. The laying of a foundation stone of a new breakwater which was to guard the vulnerable

In April 1903, Edward VII reviews the British fleet in the Grand Harbour.

entrance to the Grand Harbour afforded the occasion. With the wind from certain quarters the fleet was exposed to storms, but even more dangerous was the threat of torpedo attack from fast torpedo boats which might penetrate the screen of observation and contact mines. The torpedo was a British invention, devised by Robert Whitehead in 1866 and first offered for sale two years later. This initial steel fish had a speed of about six knots but was somewhat unmanageable until gyroscopic control was introduced after 1895 to correct it on its path so that it ran true to the target. The coastal mines were introduced after about 1885 to increase the depth of defence and prevent striking vessels from getting within torpedo range of their targets. Five years after the King's visit, his brother, the Duke of Connaught, was appointed Commander-in-Chief and High Commissioner in the Mediterranean area, so establishing the importance of our fleet in the Middle Sea and the crucial role of Malta. The fleets of France, Italy, and particularly Germany were being built up, a growing threat to British control of the sea lanes of the world. In the 1880's submarines armed with the newly invented Whitehead torpedo began to appear in the navies of Europe. In 1902 the British

Red pillar-boxes and telephone kiosks
stand like strange intruders in an alien
townscape.

navy commissioned its first submarine and in 1905 the Germans followed
suit. Thus began the development of a weapon which was to have a crucial
influence on the progress of wars and seriously to threaten Britain's confidence based upon the power of the capital ship.

The first world war came and went leaving Malta an island in isolation
far from the battle fronts. Its main value was as a supply base and a hospital
in healthy climate for the wounded of Gallipoli, hence the reference to her
as 'Nurse of the Mediterranean'.

The manufactured goods from Britain, long used on the island, still occasionally strike a visitor with their incongruity. The red pillar-boxes and Sir
Giles Gilbert Scott's cast iron telephone kiosks stand like strange intruders
in an alien townscape. Everywhere the names of the little bars that open on
to the street record association with the army and the navy, such homely,
well-known names and phrases and memories of England – 'The Union Jack',
'Joe's Bar', 'Bonzo', 'England's Glory'. Other needs were also catered for

'The Gut' in Valletta comes alive at night.

in the long, steep, narrow street called by generations of sailors 'The Gut'. As long ago as 1554 an Italian writer had realistically pointed to the need for streets such as Strada Stretta. 'The brothel', he wrote, 'and similar taverns should be placed as near as possible to the main square but carefully camouflaged.'[22]

The most nostalgic memory of Britain can be found in the tombstones of the young soldiers who gave their lives serving in this distant country. Cholera made no exception of Malta and a serious outbreak of the plague occurred in 1813. Enteric fever carried in the milk of goats once claimed many a victim as witnessed by the lonely graves in the garrison cemetery at Fort Chambray.

[1] Quotations from Nelson's letters are taken from Dane (Clemence). *The Nelson Touch* (London 1942).

[2] Most of the information on the Franco-Maltese War is taken from Laferla (A. V.) *British Malta* (Malta 1946). Its two volumes are an inexhaustible guide to the events of the British occupation, and from Zammit (Themistocles). *Malta* (Valletta 1929).

[3] Rees (William). *A History of the Order of St John of Jerusalem in Wales and on the Welsh Border* (Cardiff 1947), page 87.

[4] Mifsud (A.) *Knights Hospitallers of the Venerable Tongue of England in Malta* (Malta 1916), page 77 *et seq.*

[5] Public Record Office. W.O. 33. 8. *Malta, 28th May, 1859, Extracts.*

[6] P.R.O. W.O. 33.8. *Report on the State of the Fortress of Malta* (Valletta, 3 June 1859). *Project of Defence*, page 736 *et seq.*

[7] P.R.O. W.O. in letters. Volume 512 (19 January 1853), *letter from Governor to the Duke of Newcastle.*

[8] P.R.O. W.O. in letters. Volume 513. *Papers relating to Malta – 1854–5 Military.*

[9] P.R.O. W.O. 33/32, page 8.

[10] P.R.O. W.O. in letters. Volume 513. *Papers relating to Malta, 1854–5 Military*, page 81.

[11] P.R.O. W.O. 33. *Report on the State of the Fortress of Malta* (Valletta 3 June 1859), *on Armament*, page 90.

[12] P.R.O. W.O. 33/25. *New Works for Heavy Armaments*, page 2.

[13] P.R.O. W.O. 33/32. *Memorandum on the Defences of Malta* (23 February 1878), page 3.

[14] P.R.O. W.O. 33/25. *Report on Malta by Brig. General Adye, C.B. Director of Artillery and Stores* (December 1872).

[15] P.R.O. W.O. 33/32. *Memorandum on the Defences of Malta* (23 February 1878), page 1.

[16] Porter (M. Gray) and Weber (B. Clarke). 'Malta in 1885' in *Melita Historica*, Volume 4, No.1 (1964), page 30.

[17] Harrison and Hubbard. *Valletta and the Three Cities* (Valletta 1945) Appendix A, page xiii.

[18] Colvin (H. M.) 'Victorian Malta' in *Architectural Review* (June 1946), pages 179–180.

[19] Howling (G. J.) 'The Musta Church of Malta' in *Architectural Review* Volume 39 (January 1916), pages 15–16.

[20] Samut-Tagliaferro (A.) 'Malta's Royal Opera House' in *Sunday Times of Malta* (12 December 1965).

[21] Sultana (Donald). 'Coleridge in Malta' in *Sunday Times of Malta* (11 November 1956).

[22] *I quattro primi libri di Pietro Cataneo Senese* (Venice 1554), Book I, chapter 6, page 8r.

260

Chapter 10: The Second Siege

An aircraft pen made of rough stone walls and petrol tins filled with sand.

Throughout the twenties and thirties of this century conditions in Malta changed little from year to year, for the British garrison and fleet continued to plod the slow pattern of a conservative tradition and so the nation came to face the onslaught of a major war ill-prepared for the consequences. As the story of the second siege of Malta has been often told, it need not be recounted in great detail here. However, the general picture of the defensive position is important as it relates to the whole history of this fortress. When the Germans overran France and Italy joined in the war against Great Britain the inadequate defences of Malta faced a new threat, for the island lay vulnerable, a mere 100 miles south of the Sicilian coast. The Governor, Sir William Dobbie, wrote – 'A fortress is intended to prove its worth in days of adversity, and when the local military situation is unfavourable.'[1] In 1940 this was an understatement, for the position was more than un-favourable. The troops and munitions were much needed elsewhere as the British life-line was stretched to its limit. Malta had no aircraft either for defence or attack. She had coast guns sufficient to protect the harbours from a large-scale attack but too slow-firing to repulse a sudden, fast-moving assault, and her anti-aircraft guns were too few to cover the naval base and the airfields. Many in authority assumed that it would be impossible to operate airfields so close to the Italian mainland. How wrong they were! But General Dobbie summed up the situation with clarity: 'It must, of course, be remembered that Malta's *raison d'être* was, and is, and always will be, offensive, rather than defensive.'[2] The reason for protecting and maintaining her was to provide a forward base, an unsinkable aircraft-carrier from which to attack the Axis convoys ferrying troops and munitions across to North Africa and later to form a springboard for the invasion of the soft under-belly of Europe. On his appointment to Malta, Air Vice-Marshal Maynard discovered four fighter aircraft packed in cases in an obscure naval storeroom. These were soon uncrated and three made ready for operations against the Macchi fighters of the Italian air force. These were the famous Gloster Gladiators, christened *Faith*, *Hope*, and *Charity*, which outwitted many a faster enemy plane by their ability to turn sharply away from any impending attack. The old bi-plane construction scored its last victory. The exploits of these three planes became legendary.

Four dangers threatened Malta. Aerial bombardment might destroy the airfields, the naval dockyards, anchorages, and the morale of the civil population. Second, there was a chance of naval attack, with the ever-present danger of ships breaking into the Grand Harbour and destroying the British ships at anchor. For generations this had been one of the main threats to Malta. Third, there was the war of attrition – a blockade which would cut off food and medical supplies, and the reinforcement of troops and munitions. And fourth the possibility of invasion – an all out assault on the island with the aim of capturing it. All four methods of attack were either tried or contemplated by the Axis forces. The Italians began with aerial bombardment, first using high-level attack with formations of bombers which in good weather conditions were extremely vulnerable to the anti-aircraft defences. Fascist communiqués were intended more as an encouragement to Italian morale than as a strict statement of facts for, soon after their entry into the war, they issued a communiqué stating that 'we have destroyed all military objectives in Malta'.

The preparations for defence slowly took shape. After the personal intervention of Sir Winston Churchill a convoy destined for Singapore was diverted towards Malta in July 1941. It entered the Mediterranean supported by warships, battle cruisers and carriers of H. Force which safeguarded its passage until, nearing Cape Bon in Tunisia, the Task Force sheered off to the north to carry out a diversionary attack on the Italians. From then on, until the remnants reached Malta, the convoy was subjected to incessant attack from torpedo-bombers and light naval craft.

The garrison now formed three brigades with five battalions deployed in the north, three in the centre of the island, and six in the south. Gozo was left undefended. There were three Maltese regiments in the field and most of the British battalions were regulars, stiffened with National Service officers and men. The fixed coastal defences were augmented with quick-firing guns, Bofors and Erlikons, multiple pom-poms capable of throwing out a barrage of light tracer shells. Two regular field artillery regiments equipped with eighteen- and twenty-five-pounder guns were deployed in concealed concrete emplacements at vulnerable points around the coast and covering the three main airports. There were five regiments of artillery in the heavy anti-aircraft brigade, equipped mainly with 3·7 inch quick-firing guns, and three light anti-aircraft regiments using the Swedish Bofors gun which fired tracer shells from clips so that, rather like a rifle, several cartridges could be placed on to the gun at a time. These were the resources for defence. The defensive role, however, was auxiliary to the offensive role of Malta. For offensive purposes there were a Fleet Air Arm base at Hal Far where slow Fairy 'Swordfish' torpedo-bombers operated with good success against enemy shipping; Luqa airfield from which Wellington bombers of the Royal Air Force operated; and Ta Kali, the fighter airfield, where Hurricanes were soon brought in to replace the exhausted Gladiators, the Hurricanes in turn being supplanted by Spitfires early in May 1942. The aircraft carrier HMS *Illustrious* used the Grand Harbour in 1941, but because of the threat from German dive-bombers, which had moved into the southern Italian airfields, the main units of the Mediterranean fleet were moved to safer anchorages in Egypt. Except for the occasional visit of escort cruisers and destroyers bringing in the convoys and the shuttle service by the fast mine-laying cruisers operating from Gibraltar, from then on the main naval task lay in operating the submarines from the bomb-proof concrete pens below Fort Manoel so that these ships could create havoc in the crowded shipping lanes between Italy and the North African coast.

The first attacks came soon after the Italian entry into the war in the form of aerial bombardment, often indiscriminate and often ill-judged – even incendiary bombs were dropped on non-combustible Malta. The pace quickened when the Germans began to use their Junkers 87 (Stukas) and Junkers 88 dive-bombers with great effect on the three main objectives, the Harbour, Ta Kali and Luqa airports. To defend these points three anti-aircraft barrages were evolved, only one of which could be brought into operation as the actual attack developed. A wall of steel shrapnel and tracer filled the air with a block of explosion over the threatened position. The pace of the battle quickened, supplies ran short, anti-aircraft ammunition was rationed and food was scarce. In March 1942 two convoys set off from opposite ends of the Mediterranean in an attempt to bring much needed supplies to Malta. After being attacked in devastating fashion, the one from the east turned back, but the remnants of the convoy from Gibraltar broke through to the Grand Harbour only to be sunk at anchor by German dive-bombers. On 24 March a young lieutenant recorded in his diary: 'The heaviest raids yet experienced since I arrived. JU 88's seemed to fill the sky as they attacked the Grand Harbour. Some of them were very low and were engaged by U-type projectors. These guns threw bunches of white parachutes into the air and at first sight I imagined that the Germans were using paratroops. After lunch, formations of Stukas, escorted by fighters, attacked Safi and Hal Far, sometimes diving at angles of about eighty degrees and wriggling about all over the air.' By April 2000 alerts had been sounded as the island was pounded hourly by German and Italian bombs, but by May the tide of battle was beginning to turn. A strong reinforcement of Spitfires arrived and the *Times of Malta* wrote 'The last two days have seen a metamorphosis in the battle of Malta. After two days of the fiercest aerial combat that has ever taken place over the island, the Luftwaffe, with its Italian lackeys, has taken the most formidable beating that has been known since the Battle of Britain two and a half years ago, indeed in proportion to the numbers of aircraft involved this trouncing is even greater than the Germans suffered at that time.' On Sunday, 10 May, twenty-two German aircraft were shot down, a further twenty probably destroyed, and twenty-one others damaged. This was the beginning of the end of the air assault on Malta.

There was a time when Britain lost naval supremacy in the Mediterranean. The demands in the Far East, the pressure of the German U-boats in the Atlantic, and the sinking of two British battleships by Italian under-water saboteurs had seriously upset the position. In the circumstances, it was strange that the Italian fleet did not attempt an all out assault on Malta. Italy had the ships to bombard Valletta, but her admirals later complained that they were denied the necessary fuel to leave port by their German allies. Thus the only naval assault was a sudden spirited and totally unsuccessful attack on the Grand Harbour on the night of 26 July 1941. The Italian aim was to penetrate the Grand Harbour and sink there the merchantmen and naval ships which had just arrived in convoy from Gibraltar.

Special forces of the Italian navy had been preparing for many months and now the attacking vessels led stealthily in under cover of the darkness. The first two 'pigs', baby submarines with a detachable explosive bow and a crew of two men, crept forward below the surface searching for the submarine nets which guarded the entrance to the Grand Harbour. The aim was to blast a hole through these nets which hung beneath the twin arched girder-bridge adjoining the breakwater to Fort St Elmo. With the nets breached, fast motor torpedo boats would dash through the gap and into the Grand Harbour where amidst the general alarm it was hoped that they could create havoc among the anchored ships. Simultaneously a breach was to be made in the defences of Marsamxett and attacks made on the submarines and destroyers. The Italians were dogged by bad luck from the start. The pigs disappeared into the darkness and were never seen again. Anxiously the task commander waited for the explosions which would announce the completion of the first stage of the operation. Precious minutes slipped by, until at 4.43 am he aimed his own motor boat at the outer span of the viaduct, locked the steering and jettisoned himself into the sea. The ship struck with a violent explosion that rocked the island, but instead of clearing the gap it brought down on to itself the iron girders of the viaduct sealing more securely the gap into the Grand Harbour. Meanwhile, the coast defences had been alerted and went into action. Searchlights flashed across the sea and the tracer shells of the quick-firing guns ricocheted onto the now exposed Italian E boats. To add to their discomfort Hurricanes took off from Ta Kali and pounded the attackers with their cannon. A failure was turned into a disaster as one by one the Italian ships stopped and exploded.[3]

The work of attrition was a slow affair, but as the months went by the blockade began to have its effect. Food and drink, plentiful in the summer of 1941, became desperately short in 1942 and many of the civilians were reduced to meagre meals obtained from the Victory kitchens. Nor were the troops' rations adequate and some other ranks had to be laid off heavy work because of the shortage. As the pounding from the air continued, the irreplaceable store of anti-aircraft shells grew smaller, troop positions were often reduced to fighting with one gun while three lay idle. Fighter planes were flown in from aircraft-carriers but their fuel was desperately short. The necessities of life were running out. The fight to replenish the island was a long bitter affair, with the agony of sunken ships Britain could not afford to lose, and the anxious months of waiting as stocks grew low. Of the convoys that fought their way through to the island, two at least should receive notice. On 23 March 1942 the remnants of a convoy, three merchantmen, a cruiser, and ten destroyers, entered the safety of the Maltese harbours after a continuous pounding through the Mediterranean. The naval supply-ship *Breconshire* had been hit and her steering severely damaged, so that she made way only with the greatest difficulty. It was clear that she would not reach farther than the great bay of Marsaxlokk, and as she slowly struggled in, a screen of field guns moved up to ring the bay against enemy coastal attack, and new anti-aircraft positions were quickly established. But it was all to no avail. As the precious ship beached in the sandy waters of the bay the sky filled with the roar of Stukas – a steady stream of bombs trounced the *Breconshire* until she was a total wreck. Then the Germans switched their attention to the Grand Harbour and the light naval anchorages at Marsamxett, and the three merchantmen that had fought so hard to get there were sunk at their moorings.

Attempts to get through in June were unsuccessful, and it was not until August 1942 that the Santa Marija convoy sailed through a wall of fire to deliver in safety its cargo of aviation fuel and other necessities. Convoy WS 2S, consisting of fourteen merchant ships, slipped past the Pillars of Hercules and, entering the Mediterranean, picked up its escort of three aircraft-carriers, two battleships, six cruisers, one anti-aircraft cruiser, and twenty-four destroyers – a formidable force. As the passage of the Mediterranean narrowed towards the coast of Sicily the heavy units of the Gibraltar task force left the convoy, which proceeded to Malta protected by a naval screen of four cruisers and twelve destroyers. In the opening battle the aircraft-carrier *Eagle* had been sunk by torpedoes from a German submarine, the carrier *Indomitable* put out of action, and a merchantman and destroyer both sunk. When the naval force split, the enemy concentrated its attack on the merchant ships and their escort. By 12 August two heavy cruisers had been hit and forced to withdraw, and *Manchester*, the remaining large ship, sunk. Four more merchantmen went to the bottom. And so the disastrous thinning-out continued. The vital tanker *Ohio* was hit and disabled

The damaged tanker *Ohio* reaches the Grand Harbour.

and other cargo boats sunk. But somehow the remnants got through. At 4.30 pm on the afternoon of 13 August *Port Chalmers*, *Melbourne Star*, and the damaged *Rochester Castle*, entered the Grand Harbour, followed two days later by the *Brisbane Star* and the *Ohio*, whose heroic story of a fight for survival is now part of history. At times she was a sheet of flame from stem to stern, but when her battered hulk was finally towed into the Grand Harbour by a destroyer and two mine-sweepers, she still contained vital fuel for the air-strike against Rommel's supply line.[4] When Montgomery mounted his attack at El Alamein and broke through Rommel's lines a mere fortnight lay between life and death for the island of Malta.

In addition to attacks on the island by air and naval units, and the gauntlet run by convoys, there was a fourth menace: invasion. In the summer of 1942 the German first and second airborne divisions were moved down to southern Italy in preparation for an attack on Malta, to destroy that hornets' nest which had stung too many of the vessels supplying Rommel's Afrika Corps. The German High Command was, however, short of information. Italian frogmen swimming off the coast on dark nights in an attempt to assess the value of the underwater obstacles met with little success. A Maltese spy was landed on the island after being coached in Italy but was soon captured and shot. Of the two German reconnaissance parties known to have made a landing, one was captured and the other returned to Italy without information. The Germans and Italians were planning in the dark. They knew that the airborne invasion of Crete had been a bitter affair and the island hard won. Malta was smaller and its defences more compact. Its fields were ringed by high stone walls, an added hazard to a parachute landing, and the garrison was well prepared and ready for the battle. The plan was to drop an experimental parachute battalion east of Zurrieq and there to form a bridgehead. Six hours later the two German airborne divisions were to land in the area of the airports of Luqa and Hal Far, and two Italian divisions were to make seaborne landings at Birzebbuga in the large bay on the southeast of the island.[5] Meanwhile in Africa, Tobruk fell, and Rommel's army advanced into Egypt. Victory seemed within their grasp and this would remove the need to undertake the perilous airborne invasion of Malta. When the tide again turned against Germany, the opportunity was lost.

Apart from the devastation, the visual reminders on Malta of the second world war are less in evidence than those of earlier wars. Perhaps some sectors of the Maginot Line, the Siegfried Line and the German Western Wall, with their massive concrete bunkers and shell-proof shelters, may prove worthy of preservation so that future generations may see the living picture of a part of the world's great struggle, but in Malta the actual fortifications seem paltry when compared to those of the Baroque era. They consisted of scattered infantry pill-boxes constructed in reinforced concrete, cubic in shape and not dissimilar from the surrounding Maltese farmhouses, with sheer plain walls pierced only by the narrow slits through which the bren guns once poked. Some pill-boxes still remain. The anti-aircraft gun positions were largely sandbagged emplacements and have long since disappeared, and on the airfields the pens which gave protection from blast and flying

An infantry pill-box constructed during the second world war.

splinters to the Wellingtons, Swordfish, Hurricanes and Spitfires have all been cleared away. They consisted of walls constructed of metal petrol cans filled with sand and the cans soon rusted and were removed. The coastal gun positions added during the war were small, insignificant shelters, roofed over with a well-camouflaged shell of concrete.

The history of fortifications is a history of the development of the art of concealment, dispersion, and the ability to sink defences deeper and deeper into the ground. So it is understandable in a world of monuments that medieval castles should provide the most bulky and memorable evidence of man's aggressive spirit. The defence systems of the twentieth century, though the most powerful so far conceived, leave behind least evidence of their existence.

[1] Dobbie (Sir William G. S.) 'The Siege of Malta 1940–42' in *Royal Engineers Journal*, Volume 57 (1943), pages 1–8.

[2] Dobbie (Sir William G. S.) 'The Defence of Malta' in *Journal of the Royal United Service Institution*. Volume 87 (November 1942), pages 283-93.

[3] Ferro (H.) 'War-time Attack on Grand Harbour', letter in *Sunday Times of Malta* (8 January 1967).

[4] 'The Santa Marija Convoy' in *Sunday Times of Malta* (8 August 1965).

[5] 'Flashback to World War Two – German Brigadier discusses plan to capture Malta' in *Sunday Times of Malta* (10 August 1967).

Chapter 11: The Present Situation

After the war, Britain fulfilled her promise to restore self-government to Malta. The first step, a new constitution, was established in 1946 and in the years that followed the whole system of Commonwealth defence was revised in the light of the development of modern warfare. Malta, it was realized, had lost much of her strategic importance as the range of weapons increased and the crucial character of the Mediterranean diminished. With her changed role, the habits of lifetimes changed. The naval dockyard, the most important source of employment, was transferred to private ownership and the run-down of the British armed forces began. Independence was granted on 21 September 1964 and Malta faced her new-found freedom from generations of colonial rule with both a feeling of joy and a realization of the need to re-plan her economy. But this book is primarily concerned with the visual implications of historical events rather than a detailed description of the events themselves.

A long conservative classical tradition should be treated with respect, and the Maltese, quick to change and adapt themselves when the need arises, do treat their past with respect. In architecture, classical design has persisted into our own day, hardly broached by the intrusion of Gothic Revival. Large new churches have continued to be built in the classical style, and the result has provided a homogeneous character to the buildings of Malta and Gozo. Fortunately, a number of gifted designers have worked in this traditional style, some merely copying the work of the past, but others, with a more individual bent, able to provide a lively extension to the trappings of classicism. The parish church at Hamrum illustrates this continuity of

style. The building is a free adaptation of numberless styles with overtones of classic. The interior is all white to the cornice level and has a richly
painted quadripartite vaulted ceiling, its ribs of white picked out in filigree
gilt and its panels painted in dark blue overlaid with richly coloured pic-
tures. The gilding and the colours are effectively used – the whiteness of
the walls accentuating the verticality of the nave while one's eyes are drawn
to the richly decorated vault. Externally the church is equally singular. The
dome is a hemi-circle of silver, pleated with close-spaced plain stone ribs.
The main façade, twin towers between a pedimented centre-piece, is an
ingenious inter-weaving of Classical and Gothic motifs as though the western
towers of Leon cathedral had been married to the front of S. Maria della

Salute in Venice. It is an architectural solution which, in analysis, one would hardly expect to be successful, but which is, nevertheless, from appearance a design commanding respect. The bulk of the building is nineteenth century, but the double-skinned dome is by Guzé Damato, completed in 1958 five years before he died. Damato was born of Maltese parents in Sfax, a town in eastern Tunis, in the year 1886. At 19 he was in Malta but returned to Tunis to complete his architectural studies. From 1924 he was occupied mainly in Malta, where he designed a number of individual, robust churches in the classical style. It is to men like Damato that the credit must go for maintaining a tradition palatable to Malta until she produces a generation of architects capable of adapting modern architecture to the environmental conditions of the central Mediterranean.

In 1924 Damato began the vast parish church of Christ the King at Paola. The church has twin dome-topped towers supporting a porticoed front. The theme is basically classical, but Damato introduces a predilection for arches springing from columns which give the building a Romanesque effect. This feature occurs both on the aisle elevations and in the interior. The interior is impressive. An expansive ambulatory encircles the semicircular apse, continuing the theme of arch on column, its roof spaces domed and

A converted farmhouse at Bahar ic-caghaq.

subtly lit from windows in the drum. The proportions are tall, leading the eye to the ribbed dome which rises from a peripteral colonnade over the crossing. The dome climbs, tier upon tier, accentuating the height to its lantern. This is a strange and individual combination of motifs drawn from the classical and medieval worlds and used in a most unclassical way.

Damato's most interesting project is at Xewkija in Gozo where in 1952 he began the Rotunda, a large new parish church dedicated to St John the Baptist. The dome is some 245 feet high and has an internal diameter of 82 feet. During construction, the shell of the new church weaves a cocoon around its smaller predecessor which, on the completion of the Rotunda, will be demolished and extracted through the doors leaving a new clear internal space capable of seating a congregation of some 4000. In style the new building is Venetian Baroque, modelled on the Salute, but with sufficient variation on the theme to exercise Damato's ingenuity.

In Malta one finds more care lavished on the churches than elsewhere in the world. Nearly all are beautifully maintained, spotlessly clean, scrubbed, polished, gilded and painted. They are used throughout the week as places of worship, and have not yet become the sepulchral monuments they are elsewhere in Europe.

The persistence of the Renaissance style when well executed is infinitely preferable to the production of bad examples of modern architecture. Fortunately, much of the rebuilding on important bomb-damaged sites has been carried out in the former style. In November 1943, with the dust of war barely settled and in circumstances not dissimilar from those in which Laparelli found himself in 1565, the English architects Harrison and Hubbard were called in to put forward their plan for Valletta and the Three Cities. The plan was presented in 1945 and envisaged the now completed rebuilding of Senglea, the construction of a colonnaded Renaissance square in front of St John's co-cathedral in Valletta and a similar colonnaded treatment to the main road through Floriana. In each case the scale is big, appropriately monumental, and not dissimilar from parts of Bologna. Already the stone has mellowed and the buildings have become absorbed into their setting. Harrison and Hubbard were sensitive architects who reacted sympathetically to the indigenous architecture of Malta describing how the 'clear-cut three-dimensional forms of the rural houses are pregnant with suggestion and strangly in accord with the spirit of the age'. 'It is often

the quality of simple things', they wrote, 'which makes or mars the appearance of a city.' The simplicity in form of the rebuilt areas of bomb damaged Malta is theirs, though the architecture itself, in sympathetic vein, was designed by others.

In 1911 a Royal Commission had reported that, 'a sudden withdrawal of the British fleet and garrison would reduce a large section of the population to idleness and starvation'. With independence and the shift in the priorities of military strategy it looked as though the prediction might come true. So Malta turned rapidly to explore new avenues of trade. New light industry was established, often housed in well-designed government factories, and the main shift of attention was concentrated on the tourist industry. As a consequence Malta has seen in the last ten years the greatest building boom in her history, which in turn has forced a need to face the problems of a dying trade. The stonemason, though still active in Malta, is losing his position in the forefront of the building industry as wages rise and the shortage of good building stone begins to take effect. Slowly the cost of building houses in stone has been rising above the cost of using concrete blocks. New materials are forcing a new aesthetic which will need time to be assimilated into the Maltese scene. No longer is there a structural need for thick, robust walls, which give so much character to past building. One local architect has remarked, 'we are in danger of losing in one generation what we gained in nine centuries'. But the situation is not without hope. Modern architecture is not incompatible and a number of new buildings have shown that it is possible to shape modern architecture so that it fits sympathetically into the pattern of local requirements. Local colours are earth-brown, dust-yellow, olive-green; traditional forms are rectangular cubes pierced by small openings to restrict the entry of sun and dust. Buildings in the past have been grouped in tight compact masses for protection from the elements and the preservation of that most precious commodity, land. If architects and clients can reject undesirable foreign clichés and retain those features which are both indigenous and applicable today, then the unique character of Malta, which is its greatest attraction, can be retained. This happy marriage of old and new is shown best in the work of the young Maltese architect Richard England. He was trained in Malta, and later worked for Ponti in Milan. The building boom, caused by the expansion of the tourist industry, has given him his great opportunity. In the last few years he has designed and built numerous modern hotels and houses for expatriate settlers on the island. In a series of articles he has crystallized his thoughts on the direction which modern architecture should take in Malta. 'Architectural thought', he writes, 'proceeds through a series of simple gestures dominated by a sure instinct and talent, and born of an ancestral attachment to the land and its heritage. From this will arrive an architecture, which, since it was created under various similar requisites (environment, climatic conditions, and at times, materials), will of necessity pertain to our islands.' His own buildings imply sculptured forms which suggest a relationship with the indigenous architecture of the islands. In the scooped-out curves of the church of St Joseph at Manikata one is reminded of the ovular ruins of the Megalithic temples. Semicircular forms mirror each other across a central space and the curved form is interwoven in the complex organization of the plan. In the commodious villa la Maltija, which was built near Gharghur, the impression is one of solidity. Massive walls curved and banked from the perpendicular are reminiscent of the strength of the Maltese fortifications. Always he plays for a predominance of solid over void, and openings in the walls are reduced to the minimum – deep-set eyes in solid masonry. His work is successful because he is able to combine a respect for the vernacular architecture of the past characterized by the simple cubic forms of the clusters of farmhouse building and, those masterpieces of skilled relationships, the conglomeration of cubes and clean-cut sculptural units which pile up to give so distinctive a silhouette to the Maltese villages, with a reinterpretation of Baroque design. England is an architectural sculptor with a respect for the past and an admiration for the present. But he is also a realist, warning against the explosive situation which exists in Malta. He writes, 'the size of our islands does not allow us the possibility of error. In fact, a few mistakes will be more than is required to produce a general impression of failure.' Already the sun-seekers are here in their thousands clamouring for accommodation in the Sterling Area, seeking out the advantages of a lower cost of living and a warm and pleasant climate, features which combine to make Malta one of the most attractive propositions for British property buyers. The pressure is on and already the building industry is showing signs that it cannot cope with the demand. But the delicate balance is by no means lost as many people do their best to create an improvement in the environment along with an expansion of trade. The Government and numerous private individuals have sensed the danger of the situation. Planning legislation is being enacted and town planning recommendations are being put through for both Malta and Gozo. The Council of Europe has agreed on a pilot scheme to produce an inventory of historic and architectural monuments on the island, and *Din L'Art Helwa*, the Maltese Civic Trust, has been set up to act as a watch-dog for the heritage of the islands.

Malta has many assets. Her climate makes her an ideal holiday island. There is good bathing and boating in her calm blue sea and her numerous creeks and harbours. The richness of her history is manifested in her architecture and, above all, in her fortifications and defensive works whose romantic and evocative nature has not always been fully appreciated locally. Her monuments are more thickly clustered on the ground than almost anywhere else in the world and lie close to her beaches accessible to those who wish to combine in their holiday a variety of experiences.

Index